The Outbreak of the
First World War

Praeger Studies in Diplomacy and Strategic Thought

The Development of RAF Strategic Bombing Doctrine, 1919–1939
Scot Robertson

The Outbreak of the First World War

Strategic Planning, Crisis Decision Making, and Deterrence Failure

JOHN H. MAURER

Praeger Studies in Diplomacy and Strategic Thought
B.J.C. McKercher, Series Editor

Westport, Connecticut
London

Library of Congress Cataloging-in-Publication Data

Maurer, John H.
    The outbreak of the first World War : strategic planning, crisis
decision making, and deterrence failure / John H. Maurer.
        p.   cm. — (Praeger studies in diplomacy and strategic thought,
ISSN 1076–1543)
    Includes bibliographical references and index.
    ISBN 0–275–94998–2 (alk. paper)
    1. World War, 1914–1918. 2. Strategy. I. Title.
D521.M455   1995
940.3—dc20   95–22012

British Library Cataloguing in Publication Data is available.

Library of Congress Catalog Card Number: 95–22012
ISBN: 0–275–94998–2
ISSN: 1076–1543

First published in 1995

Praeger Publishers, 88 Post Road West, Westport, CT 06881
An imprint of Greenwood Publishing Group, Inc.

Printed in the United States of America

The paper used in this book complies with the
Permanent Paper Standard issued by the National
Information Standards Organization (Z39.48–1984).

10 9 8 7 6 5 4 3 2 1

Contents

Acknowledgments

I incurred a great many debts while completing this book. First, I would like to mention the intellectual debt that I owe Donald Kagan of Yale University. His approach to examining the outbreak of the Peloponnesian War was instrumental in shaping my thinking about how wars begin. He is an inspiring teacher, and his influence can be detected in countless ways throughout this book. At the Fletcher School of Law and Diplomacy, the late John Roche played an instrumental part in helping me finish this book. His careful reading of the manuscript provided me with a thoughtful commentary that markedly improved the final version. I am deeply indebted to him for encouraging me to write this book. He will be sorely missed by those who worked with him. I also want to thank Professor Robert L. Pfaltzgraff, Jr. for reading the manuscript. His suggestions about ways to sharpen the book's analytical conclusions have greatly strengthened it. When he still taught at the Fletcher School, Professor Uri Ra'anan provided me with insightful suggestions about ways to approach the study of military planning in Austria-Hungary. I must note that the International Security Studies Program of the Fletcher School supported my research, and I am grateful for this assistance.

In writing this study, I received much helpful advice from Dennis Showalter, Bradley J. Meyer, Michael Vlahos, and Erik Goldstein. They generously agreed to read earlier versions of this manuscript, and their judicious criticism made this a much better book. Their encouragement helped me to see this book through to completion. I am also very grateful to the guidance I received from Brian McKercher. I especially appreciate his encouragement to submit this study for consideration in the book series he edits on strategy.

My colleagues in the Policy and Strategy Department of the Naval War College in Newport, Rhode Island, deserve my special thanks. I am particularly grateful for the support I received from George Baer, chairman of the department. His support reduced the burdens of readying the book for publication. His predecessor as department chairman, William C. Fuller, Jr. also backed me in undertaking this project and made preparing the first draft of the book much easier. Meanwhile, Alberto Coll, Michael Handel, David Kaiser, Brad Lee, Doug Porch, and Steve Ross have shaped and refined my views about strategy during the First World War. My colleagues make the Strategy Department a terrific place to work, and I consider myself fortunate to be counted as one of their number. At the Naval War College Library, I want to thank Ms. Alice Juda and Ms. Robin Lima, who so ably assisted me in my research.

My family has been a constant source of support for me during the time it took me to finish this book. My sister Margaret Maurer helped me in carrying out my research, and I am extremely grateful to her. I also want to thank my parents for their love and support over the years. They encouraged me in my studies and greatly eased the burden of my work. It is my deep regret that this book did not appear before my father passed away. This work is dedicated to my parents.

Finally, I am most especially mindful of the contribution made by my wife Maureen. With her patience, good humor, and love, Maureen sustained me throughout the writing of this book, helping me to finish. She is my best friend and my love. My children, Johnny, Margaret, and James, also played an important part in helping me to complete this book by countenancing my protracted stays in the study working on the computer.

Abbreviations

AMD	Conrad, *Aus Meiner Dienstzeit*
B.D.	*British Documents on the Origins of the War*
D.D.	*Die Deutschen Dokumente zum Kriegsausbruch*
KA, GenStab, OpB	Files of the Operations Bureau, General Staff, Kriegsarchiv, Vienna
MKFF	Militärkanzlei Franz Ferdinand, Kriegsarchiv, Vienna
ÖU	*Österreich-Ungarns Aussenpolitik*
ÖULK	*Österreich-Ungarns letzter Krieg*
Ratzenhofer MSS	Ratzenhofer manuscript collection, Hoover Institution archives
Weltkrieg	*Der Weltkrieg*

Introduction

In the summer of 1914, Austria-Hungary and Germany began the First World War with large-scale military offensives. In the Balkans, Austria-Hungary's armies attacked in an attempt to overrun Serbia. On the front facing Russia, Austria-Hungary undertook another offensive in response to urgent appeals for military assistance from its ally Germany. While Austria-Hungary attacked in eastern Europe, Germany launched its own offensive drive against France. The German army attacked quickly, moving across Belgium and deep into France. Germany's military leaders aimed at nothing less than delivering a knockout blow to the French army in the initial round of fighting. These opening military moves by Austria-Hungary and Germany transformed a Balkan war into a struggle for European hegemony.

This study examines what led the leaders of Austria-Hungary and Germany to launch these offensives at the beginning of the First World War. My focus is primarily on understanding why high-risk offensive strategies were adopted during an international confrontation and how these strategies reflected the political ambitions of Austria-Hungary and Germany. This requires an examination of the strategic assessments, prewar military planning, and the decisions made during the July Crisis that led to war. In focusing on these issues, I attempt to build on the studies that have appeared during the past ten years in the fields of international relations and strategic studies on the outbreak of the First World War.

In Part One (chapters 1–3) of this study, I examine the strategic planning undertaken by the general staffs in Austria-Hungary and Germany before 1914. Military planners in both countries faced a multi-front strategic problem. They needed to apportion the forces available to them between various potential theaters of war. In Austria-Hungary's case, military planners devised contingency plans for fighting Russia, Romania, Serbia, and

Italy. The strategic nightmare of military planners in the Habsburg Monarchy was that they would have to fight a coalition that included all of these countries. As the war itself would show, this worst case assessment of fighting simultaneously on several fronts was not farfetched.

The German general staff wrestled with the strategic problem of planning for a two-front war against France and Russia. German military planners were forced to choose the front to attack, where to defend, and what balance of forces were necessary to carry out these tasks. Their solution was an audacious "win-hold-win" strategy—the famous Schlieffen Plan—in which the German army would concentrate the bulk of its strength against France in an attempt to achieve a quick victory. The German army's leadership thought that it would take only eight weeks after the order to mobilize for them to beat France. While Germany sought to win quickly against France, German forces in the eastern theater of war would defend against an expected Russian invasion. Germany's ability to carry out the Schlieffen Plan rested on the ability of German forces, supported by the armies fielded by its ally Austria-Hungary, to prevent Russia from scoring a major military success in eastern Europe. During the initial period of war, Germany's leaders wanted to postpone a military decision on the Russian front while they defeated the French army. Defensive operations against Russia thus played an integral part in German plans for an offensive campaign in France. After destroying the French army in battle, the German army would then redeploy against Russia. Only after the defeat of France could Germany mass sufficient forces in the east to defeat Russia.

My analysis of prewar planning shows that military decision makers in Austria-Hungary and Germany were not mindless "cultists," who behaved irrationally because of an addiction to offensive operations. Instead, the general staffs in both countries carefully examined and elaborated defensive strategies as well as offensive strikes. Offensives were thought of as a means to achieve a quick outcome, whereas the defense was intended to hold on a front in an attempt to delay a military decision. Military planners in Germany, for example, rejected the notion of a major offensive against Russia, in large part because they could not see how it would lead to a war-winning outcome.

Of course, the opening offensives by Austria-Hungary and Germany failed to deliver a short war. Because they failed, these offensives are often derided as reckless ventures that ignored strategic and operational realities. Yet, a close examination of the opening campaigns of the war shows that the offensive strikes launched by Austria-Hungary and Germany were not preordained to failure. France and Russia found it very difficult to defeat the attacks that were launched against them. Austria-Hungary's attack into Russia almost succeeded in encircling and annihilating a Russian army at the Battle of Komarov. Meanwhile, to frustrate the Schlieffen Plan and halt Germany's onslaught, the French army needed to make a tremendous military exertion, carry out a skillful redeployment of forces from one flank to the other, and coordinate its operations with the British army in France.

Another aspect of the prewar military planning of Austria-Hungary and Germany examined in this study is their strategic coordination. Military planners in Austria-Hungary and Germany had different strategic assumptions and operational aims. German planners wanted to win quickly over France, while Franz Conrad von Hötzendorf (Austria-Hungary's chief of staff) aimed at bringing about Serbia's downfall. Given these priorities, devising a common strategy for fighting Russia eluded military planners in both countries. Conrad wanted Germany to carry out an offensive against Russia, thus diverting the attention of Russian forces away from Austria-Hungary. German planners, however, had no intention of attacking with the forces they left behind in the East against a numerically superior Russian army. Such an attack, in their view, would be suicidal and bring no real benefit to Austria-Hungary. The German general staff did not believe blindly in offensive operations. These differences in strategic outlook prevented Austria-Hungary and Germany from settling on a common plan for the conduct of military operations.

The inability of the Central Powers to agree on a common strategy had serious repercussions. For Austria-Hungary, the result was a military debacle and crippling losses that undermined its standing as an independent great power. Better coordination between the Central Powers might have avoided exposing Austria-Hungary to the danger of a major defeat during the initial campaigns of the war.

Part Two of this study (chapters 4–8) examines the July Crisis of 1914, attempting to explain why the leaders of Austria-Hungary and Germany chose the mix of offensive and defensive strategic options that they did. The decision to attack or defend did not occur in a political vacuum. Military operations were intended to obtain major political results. The leaders of Austria-Hungary and Germany adopted offensive strategies as a way to achieve their political ambitions. Military planners sought to crush an enemy's ability to resist so that political decision makers could then impose terms on the vanquished. The 1914 offensives undertaken by Austria-Hungary and Germany thus reflected their political goals as well as the strategic doctrines of war planners.

An analysis of the Central Powers' war plans thus entails an examination of their political aims. With the attack on Serbia, Austria-Hungary's leaders wanted to crush the threat posed by Serbian nationalist aspirations. A campaign of state-sponsored terrorism, undertaken by Serbia's military intelligence service, threatened the territorial integrity of the Habsburg Monarchy. The creation of a greater Serbia entailed destroying Habsburg rule in Bosnia and seizing territory from Austria-Hungary. The leaders of Austria-Hungary viewed the assassination of the Archduke Franz Ferdinand as a provocative terrorist attack, masterminded by the Serbian military. To prevent further acts of terrorism, the Monarchy's leaders concluded that they must attack and crush the Serbian army. With the defeat of the Serbian army, Vienna intended to impose a harsh peace settlement that converted Serbia into a satellite state. Only with the complete defeat of Serbia would the Monarchy's southern frontier be made secure. The unlimited political aims of Austria-Hungary's leaders required an offensive campaign into the Balkans: a defensive strategy would not achieve the goal of rooting out the threat posed by Serbia.

The July Crisis also provided Germany's leaders with an opportunity to improve their country's security position. The German chancellor, Theobald von Bethmann Hollweg, thought that he could exploit the confrontation in the Balkans to force changes in the international line-up to Germany's benefit. First, German decision makers wanted to reassure their ally Austria-Hungary by supporting its stand against Serbia. Austria-Hungary was Germany's main ally. In the wake of a state-sponsored terrorist attack, Austria-Hungary's leaders wanted reassurance that they were not isolated within the international system. Franz Ferdinand's assassination thus posed a serious test for the alliance of Austria-Hungary and Germany. By backing their ally, Germany's leaders wanted to demonstrate their country's credibility as a coalition partner.

Second, a triumph for Austria-Hungary over Serbia might produce a bandwagon effect, as other states saw the advantages of aligning themselves more closely to Germany and Austria-Hungary. It was thought that Italy and Romania would reaffirm their support as allies of the Central Powers. Turkey, too, would want to strengthen its security ties to Germany in the aftermath of a Balkan war. Meanwhile, Bulgaria would benefit by cooperating with Austria-Hungary in keeping Serbian ambitions in check.

Third, by smashing Serbia and inducing a bandwagon effect in the Balkans, Austria-Hungary and Germany would also inflict a major defeat on Russia. Tsarist Russia had long tried to portray itself as Serbia's protector and hegemon of the Balkan states. These Russian pretensions in the Balkans would collapse with the defeat of Serbia. Austria-Hungary would then emerge triumphant in its longstanding rivalry with Russia in the Balkans.

Fourth, Bethmann Hollweg saw a chance to pry Russia apart from its entente coalition partners, France and Great Britain. German leaders doubted whether the British government would fight Germany over a confrontation that started because of a terrorist act in the Balkans. If the British government did stand aside, Britain's credibility as a coalition partner would suffer in the eyes of Russian decision makers. By highlighting the fragility of the security link between Britain and Russia, Germany might break the Triple Entente. Germany could then assume the role of balancer, putting Berlin in the enviable position of being able to play off Britain against Russia.

Finally, if Russian decision makers went ahead and forced a showdown by supporting Serbia against Austria-Hungary, Germany would have a favorable opportunity to fight Russia. Russia's rapid military recovery from the defeats it suffered in the Russo-Japanese War (1904–1905) troubled Germany's military leaders and the German chancellor Bethmann Hollweg. They feared that Russia's military buildup posed a formidable new threat to Germany's security. In their view, time was not on Germany's side. Rather than wait and face Russia when it had completed its military buildup by 1916 or 1917, Germany's military leadership and Bethmann Hollweg sought to strike first. The July Crisis gave them the opportunity.

If war came, then, the leaders of Austria-Hungary and Germany intended to change the international status quo. They expected a major war to produce dramatic changes in the international system. Austria-Hungary intended to crush Serbia and defeat Russia's aspirations in the Balkans. By smashing French fighting power, Berlin could then dictate a peace settlement that secured Germany's dominant position among the European great powers. Defensive strategies did not offer the leaders of Austria-Hungary and Germany a way to achieve the tangible results that they sought in a great-power war. Given their interest in overturning the balance of power, decision makers in Austria-Hungary and Germany turned to offensive military operations.

During the July Crisis, the contingency plans developed by staff planners were put into play. Political decision makers and military leaders had to choose from the menu of strategic options open to them, often modifying prewar plans along the way. This was most pronounced in the case of Austria-Hungary, where the evolving strategic situation called for considerable flexibility in the deployment of its military forces. Conrad initially expected to amass overwhelming force against Serbia. In Conrad's mind, Austria-Hungary's principal policy aim was the complete defeat of Serbia. To concentrate the force required to crush Serbia in a quick campaign, Conrad even went so far as to drop a proposed offensive against Russia, which he had agreed to in prewar staff talks with German military leaders. Conrad's strategy to shelve the attack against Russia in favor of an offensive strike on Serbia shocked and dismayed Germany's leaders. German military planners counted on an offensive by Austria-Hungary to tie down Russian forces long enough for Germany to execute the Schlieffen Plan. By abandoning its offensive against Russia, Austria-Hungary's actions appeared to jeopardize Germany's chances for a quick victory over France. Germany's leaders asked that the attack on Serbia be scaled down and the Russian offensive go ahead as planned. In response to the appeals from Berlin for military assistance, Austria-Hungary redeployed forces from the Serbian front to Russia, and Habsburg decision makers dropped the defensive scheme on the Russian front in favor of an offensive one. The redeployment of Austria-Hungary's forces and the attack into Russia highlight the failings of the prewar staff discussions to promote strategic cooperation.

Germany's leaders also faced a difficult choice during the July Crisis, namely whether to carry out the Schlieffen Plan or adopt a defensive strategy against France. Germany did not have to use the Schlieffen Plan in 1914. It could have split its forces more evenly between the French and Russian fronts. German forces could then await French or Russian attacks from defensive positions. Whether France or Russia would have attacked in those circumstances is by no means clear. Further, if Germany did not attack through Belgium on its way to crush France, Britain's armed intervention in the war would have been even more problematic. If Germany had abandoned the Schlieffen Plan, the First World War might have started with a "phoney war," where the major powers avoided attacking each other. Heavy fighting might then have occurred during the initial period of war only in the Balkans, a secondary theater, where Austria-Hungary and Serbia faced off against each other. By triggering Britain's intervention, the Schlieffen Plan upset Bethmann Hollweg's diplomatic attempt to split the Triple Entente. This was the greatest failing of the Schlieffen Plan.

The concluding chapter of this study explores why deterrence failed in 1914. Deterring Austria-Hungary from attacking Serbia and Germany from employing the Schlieffen Plan would have proven a difficult task for the other European great powers. Military leaders in Austria-Hungary and Germany thought the balance of military forces permitted them to carry out their offensive strikes with a reasonable chance of success. The weaknesses of the French and Russian military posture gave the Central Powers opportunities to exploit with preemptive attack strategies. In a few years, Russia's military buildup—the expansion of its army's combat strength and effectiveness, and the improvement in its ability to deploy quickly—would have promoted deterrence by closing the most important window of opportunity open to the Central Powers for offensive action. By 1914, war planners in Austria-Hungary were not sanguine about their chances for a successful offensive on the Russian front. This shift in the balance of forces led Conrad initially to put off plans for attacking Russia. If the attack was postponed, Germany's planners would also have been forced to scrap the Schlieffen Plan. Once Russia could deploy its armies to the frontiers almost as rapidly as Germany, the German army would no longer have had the time to defeat France before a powerful Russian offensive developed. In 1914, however, Russia's buildup had not progressed far enough to deter decision makers in Austria-Hungary and Germany from beginning a war with attack strategies.

To deter preemptive attacks by Austria-Hungary and Germany in 1914, Britain needed to play a more active role in promoting crisis stability. One aim of the concluding chapter is to examine the constraints that shaped British foreign policy decision making. Britain could have done little to directly influence decision making in Austria-Hungary during the July Crisis. Only Berlin could have deterred action by Austria-Hungary in 1914. Britain could have played, however, a crucial role in shaping Germany's foreign policy and strategy options. Germany's political leaders wanted to avoid a war with Britain. A hard-line foreign policy stance by Britain would have exercised a sobering effect on Germany's leaders. Even as late as August 1, when a great-power war was practically inevitable, a British warning might nonetheless have resulted in Germany's leaders dropping the Schlieffen Plan. The threat of British intervention, then, might have given pause to Germany's political leadership, forcing them to reassess their political ambitions and settle for more limited gains. By failing to deter Germany's Schlieffen Plan, Britain faced the costly alternative of having to fight offensively on the Western Front to drive back the German army from the territorial gains it made in Belgium and France during the initial campaigns. For Britain, deterrence failure would carry an extremely high price.

Part One

War Planning

Chapter 1

The Short War Dogma

When war broke out in the late summer of 1914, Kaiser Wilhelm told his soldiers heading for the front: "You will be home before the leaves have fallen from the trees."[1] Most people throughout Europe agreed with this optimistic forecast, believing that the conflict would not last longer than a few months. It is difficult to find any major political figure or military leader who dissented from this view.[2] The dogmas of political economy that then held sway—the interdependence of great power economies, the seemingly prohibitive cost of waging a modern war, the supposed limited ability of the state to intervene in a country's economic life, and the fear of social revolution—appeared to dictate the necessity of short wars in the modern era.[3] Like the campaigns of Napoleon a century earlier and the wars conducted by the Prussian General Helmuth von Moltke at the middle of the nineteenth century, the initial battles and the subsequent pursuit by the victorious army into the interior of the enemy's country would dictate the outcome of the conflict. When good armies are led by great generals, wars do not become protracted, so it was widely thought. Another factor that concerned governing elites was that, if a conflict did become bogged down in a stalemate, the result might be social revolution. War could serve as a catalyst for a revolutionary uprising of the people against the established political and social order.[4] The defeats suffered by Russia in the Russo-Japanese War of 1904–1905 sparked a revolutionary upheaval throughout the Russian empire against the tsarist regime.

Of course, forecasts of a short war were a monumental strategic miscalculation that had the most tragic consequences. This chapter examines the principal tenets of the short war dogma that exercised such a powerful hold over so many people's views about war and guided war planners before 1914. Since it was thought that any war between modern European states must be short, military planners concentrated their efforts on detailing what they saw as the ingredients for decisive success. First, staff planners drew up elaborate railway schedules to speed deployment of troops to the frontiers. Second, the general staffs and their chiefs wrote operational plans that aimed at nothing less than the destruction of an enemy's army in battle. A.J.P. Taylor is correct in saying that the great powers of this era "were, as their name implies, organizations for power, that is in the last resort for war . . . the basic test for them as Great Powers was their ability to wage war."[5] Military planners before 1914, however, narrowly defined a country's ability to wage war by the time needed for deployment, the number of artillery pieces in a division, and the total of divisions that could be placed in the field. Industrial capacity, agricultural production, and the concomitant governmental institutions to organize people and resources for a protracted conflict played next to no part in the calculations of military planners. This restricted focus of war planning precluded military planners from looking beyond the first battles and imagining the strategic contours of a protracted war. After all, a protracted conflict would test the industrial, social, and political stamina of the great powers. This kind of struggle could not be reduced to the precision of a railway schedule or the daily march rate of troops in an operations plan. Quite simply, military planners could not provide a neat operational solution to the strategic problems posed by a protracted conflict.

Instead of dwelling on contingencies that seemed problematical, war planners before 1914 concentrated on the task of securing a knockout blow to the enemy's armies in the first round—the decisive battle or battle of annihilation.[6] This "decisive battle of annihilation" would overwhelmingly dictate the outcome of the wars fought between continental European states. Bereft of its army, a continental state would have no alternative but to seek an armistice and negotiate for the best terms it could obtain to end the war. The essential component of the short war dogma, then, was the climactic battle of annihilation. At the beginning of this century military planners and commentators had a distinct type of battle in mind when they spoke of a "battle of annihilation." Annihilation meant the destruction or capture of the enemy's army. In this type of battle, the victorious side captured large numbers of prisoners, standards, and cannon. These trophies were the outward signs of the broken morale and ruptured organization of the defeated army. Captured trophies, rather than grisly "body counts," were the distinguishing feature of a successful field commander. Military theorists and war planners drew a distinction between battles that resulted in a limited victory—or what Napoleon called an "ordinary victory" and the famous strategist Carl von Clausewitz termed a simple victory—and a battle of annihilation. An ordinary victory, while it might result in the defeated army suffering heavy losses and retreating, would not produce a short war. Only a battlefield victory that destroyed an adversary's organized power for resistance, it was thought, stood any chance of bringing a quick decision. The battle of Borodino during Napoleon's Russian campaign of 1812 is perhaps the best known battle of this type. Operations planners on the general staffs thus sought to avoid fighting these types of battles and instead aimed at annihilating their opponent's army. The battle of annihilation was the solution to an operational stalemate and a protracted conflict. The culmination of the short war, then, was the battle of annihilation destroying the enemy's army. In pursuit of a short war, operational planners sought not only to avoid defeats, but "ordinary victories" as well.[7]

Since the initial battles would decide the outcome of a modern war, economic preparations for a conflict were minimal. Central banks kept stockpiles of bullion on hand, while governments wanted to provide for the country's immediate food requirements by ensuring the harvest and purchasing grain. Mobilization would disrupt the economy by tying up a country's transportation system and drawing manpower from industry. In each of the great powers, mobilization paralyzed the operations of coal mines, iron foundries, and engineering works that were vital for the production of war materiel. Only in 1915 did it become apparent that a country's ability to produce armaments required the return of workers from the front to these industries.[8]

The experience of the last major war between European great powers, the Franco-Prussian War of 1870–1871, also led war planners to discount the importance of economic considerations. In 1870 the economic positions of France and Germany were roughly equal. French heavy industry produced as much iron and steel as did the whole of Germany. Although Germany possessed a larger population, this factor was not of decisive importance since neither side completely mobilized its full manpower potential. Moreover, Fance's financial position was undoubtedly superior to that of Germany. This can readily be seen by the rapidity with which France, burdened by defeat and torn by a bloody civil war, paid off the huge indemnity that had been saddled on her by Berlin after the war. Had France's military position with regard to Germany more closely resembled its relative economic position, a rapid German victory would have been unlikely. France possessed the economic resources to carry out a much larger mobilization of military forces than what it deployed along the frontiers at the war's beginning. The scale and intensity of French resistance after the opening defeats around Metz and at Sedan reveals that France owned substantial untapped resources at the war's beginning. France mobilized considerable forces around the countryside and prolonged the conflict for another three months. The opening German victories, however, robbed France of the time it needed to exploit the military potential of its economy to expand the army. In the Franco-Prussian War, the ability to deploy superior forces during the initial battles had proved decisive.[9]

Yet the soldiers were not the only ones to carry false assumptions about economics. Many leading financiers and economists shared these views, believing that the interdependent, industrial economies of the great powers could not wage a protracted war against each other. It was widely thought that no country could afford to finance the high costs associated with maintaining modern mass armies in the field for a protracted period. In addition, the severing of trade between states by war would dislocate the economies of the belligerents and lead to their rapid economic collapse. The Austrian economic historian Eduard März has aptly noted: "Only the Great Depression has furnished similar examples of misjudgement by economic experts."[10]

To postwar historians and military commentators studying the cruel deadlock of the trenches, the focus of prewar military planners on operational issues appeared unduly narrow and far removed from the reality of the war that followed. Gerhard Ritter decried the "purely military" nature of staff planning not bound by any meaningful political guidelines or constraints.[11] Others, like Winston Churchill, appalled by the horrible slaughter caused by modern weaponry, blamed military planners for failing to take into account sufficiently the changes wrought by technological innovation.[12] Instead of delivering on their promise of a short war, the deployment plans of the general staffs were blueprints for disaster. After the war ended, parliamentarians in France investigated their general staff's inadequate prewar preparations for defending the industrial regions of Lorraine and Flanders. In writing about the disastrous failure of France's Plan XVII in 1914, Bernard Brodie remarked that this "was neither the first nor the last time that bad anthropology contributed to bad strategy."[13] It was also an instance of bad economics. The "short-war paradigm" of the French High Command had permitted the Germans to occupy these important industrial and mining areas. These territorial losses hurt French efforts to sustain a war of attrition. Yet the French were not alone in 1914: military planners in all of the European great powers failed to appreciate the importance of industrial production and technological innovation in modern warfare.[14]

These criticisms are, however, perhaps only clear with the advantage of hindsight. In his analysis of the process behind scientific inquiry and discovery, T. S. Kuhn noted that a paradigm "is declared invalid only if an alternate candidate is available to take its place. . . . The decision to reject one paradigm is always simultaneously the decision to accept another."[15] Strategic theory and military planning in the years immediately prior to the First World War exhibited a similar pattern of reasoning. There was no alternate paradigm to the dogma of the battle of annihilation. To be sure, there were some notable dissenters to the notion that the next war would be short. There was the famous warning from none other than the strategic architect of Germany's victory in the Franco-Prussian War, Helmuth von Moltke, who prophesied in his farewell speech to the German Reichstag that if "war should break out . . . it might be a Seven or even a Thirty Years' War."[16] The famous military historian and commentator Hans Delbrück also became involved in a celebrated public debate on strategy when he detailed the concept of *Ermattungsstrategie*, or strategy of attrition, which was at odds with the operational teachings of the general staff.[17]

The most extensive critique of the short war dogma appearing before 1914 was written by the Polish financier Ivan Bloch. His massive multi-volume study, entitled *The Future of War*, argued that wars between industrial societies, fought with modern weaponry, would not be decided within the course of a single campaign.[18] Bloch ridiculed the historical approach for studying war done by the general staffs in search of an operational recipe for a modern-day Cannae, Austerlitz, and Sedan. Technology had rendered obsolete such notions of operational success, making the study of the past battles irrelevant to understanding wars of the future. Bloch thought that the development of modern weaponry had reached the stage where the "soldier . . . has so perfected the mechanism of slaughter that he has practically secured his own extinction." Moreover, the growing economic interdependence of the great powers made war a form of economic suicide. If the unthinkable did happen, however, and the great powers engaged in an atavistic war with each other, Bloch predicted unprecedented slaughter and battlefield stalemate. No belligerent would win a "decisive" battle over its enemies. The resulting stalemate and heavy combat losses would only end with the economic collapse and social revolution of the belligerents. Bloch hoped that his study would prove the practical impossibility of war:

Even in the leading circles of Europe hardly anyone will dare deny that it will be possible to bring our means of annihilation to such a degree of perfection that war must become completely impossible. But the question is: have we not already reached such a stage of development in military apparatus, does the sum total of conditions not already exist under which we must eliminate war, since it has not only become a shattering experience, but also politically fruitless?[19]

A major war, then, could not be justified by any rational political purpose.

To Bloch's critics, his avowedly pacifist stance appeared naive. Delbrück argued that, despite the growing economic interdependence of states, international political rivalries would continue. Self-defense also required that the great powers keep abreast of potential adversaries. In the absence of a world government, each great power ultimately needed to protect itself from aggression. For a political realist, the best guarantee of peace remained the ability of military power to deter conflict.[20]

In 1914 statesmen and soldiers understood as well as Bloch the horrific social and political consequences of a protracted war. Theobald von Bethmann Hollweg, Germany's chancellor, did not see a general war as a way to strengthen the legitimacy of existing regimes. "On the contrary,"

Bethmann Hollweg thought, "a World War with its incalculable consequences would strengthen tremendously the power of Social Democracy,
because they [sic] preached peace, and would topple many a throne."[21] The
revolutionary upheaval that accompanied Russia's defeat in the Russo-
Japanese War provided an object lesson of what might occur to any regime
that failed in war. Since a protracted conflict would only benefit the political
Left, decision makers wanted to avoid it.

In a way unintended by Bloch, his stark portrait of the course and
consequences of future war buttressed the arguments of those who aimed
at fighting a short war, decided by a battle of annihilation. After all, the
alternative presented by Bloch highlighted the importance of achieving a
knockout blow in the first round to forestall a long war of attrition. Count
Alfred Schlieffen, the high priest of the dogma of the battle of annihilation,
emphasized this point. He believed wars of attrition "are impossible in an
age when a nation's existence is founded on the uninterrupted continuance
of its trade and industry; a rapid decision is essential if the machinery that
has been brought to a standstill is to be set in motion again. A strategy of
exhaustion is unworkable when the maintenance of millions demands the
expenditures of billions." The military operations of the Russo-Japanese
War further convinced Schlieffen of the necessity of obtaining an early
decision. During the Russo-Japanese War, the Russian and Japanese armies
fighting each other in Manchuria became bogged down in trench warfare.
Schlieffen argued: "Out there in Manchuria they may face each other for
months on end in impregnable positions. In Western Europe we cannot
allow ourselves the luxury of waging a war in this manner. The machine
with its thousand wheels, upon which millions depend for their livelihood,
cannot stand still for long. . . . We must try to overthrow the enemy quickly
and destroy him."[22] Except for pacifism or a protracted war of attrition,
there appeared no alternative to the short war paradigm propagated by the
general staffs in the continental great powers. Thus, the battle of annihilation might avert the horrors of military stalemate, economic collapse, and
political revolution.

To avoid this catastrophe, all the continental great powers assumed the
offensive in the attempt to overthrow their adversaries quickly at the
outbreak of war in 1914.[23] Russian planners devised and carried out an
amended version of the so-called Plan 19, which called for simultaneous
offensives against both Germany and Austria-Hungary.[24] French armies,
following the dictates of Joffre's Plan XVII, went onto the offensive into the
Rhineland.[25] In Austria-Hungary, Conrad committed his forces to offensives against Russia and Serbia.[26] Employing perhaps the most famous of
the pre-1914 war plans—that devised by Schlieffen and the younger
Moltke—Germany brought its armies into action by a wide sweeping
movement through Belgium intended to envelop and destroy the French
army.[27]

When all these plans failed to bring the expected rapid defeat of the enemy, the inadequacy of prewar economic preparations became readily apparent. By late October 1914, with the exhaustion of prewar stockpiles of arms and ammunition, the belligerents needed to rely upon current production. Wartime rates of consumption, however, surpassed production. This resulted in the curtailment of military operations amid talk of a "shell shortage" and a "munitions crisis." With the onset of positional warfare during the first war winter, strategy was no longer equated solely with operations plans. Since the clash of armies failed to produce a decision, the outcome of the conflict rested on the competition of the rival economies to field large armies and produce the tools of war. Modern warfare between great powers required more than the call-up and deployment of armies: it demanded the mobilization of a country's entire economic life to produce large quantities of war material. As Bloch had predicted, in a war of attrition the industrial manager would play as important a part as the military officer. Attrition was shown to be a condition of modern warfare.[28]

Mobilization meant the transition of military and naval units from their peacetime concentration of men and equipment to their war strength. At mobilization new units, not existing in peacetime, were also created, and all fortified places (fortresses, naval ports, block houses, and watch posts) were prepared to withstand an assault. In Austria-Hungary, for example, the law of 1889 established the peacetime army strength at approximately 400,000 men, or less than one percent of the total population of Austria-Hungary. On mobilization, the army expanded to 3,720,000 men, or about eight percent of the Monarchy's population.[29]

The peacetime strength of the armed forces provided only a partial picture of the military forces of the great powers. A country measured its military power not only by the size of its army in peacetime, but how rapidly its forces could mobilize and reach war strength. Military commentators at the turn of the century ascribed Prussia's victories in 1866 and 1870 to her capability to complete mobilization ahead of her opponents. In the aftermath of these wars, military reformers in the continental great powers wanted to take steps to reduce the time needed to mobilize the Monarchy's forces. For example, to ensure a rapid and orderly mobilization, in 1882 Austria-Hungary adopted a territorial system for the stationing of the army's regiments within the Monarchy. This system, based on the model of the Prussian army's cantons, divided the Monarchy into recruiting districts, which supplied men for the armed forces. Each regiment of the army was assigned a recruiting district.[30]

The regiment provided the basic building block of European armies before 1914. The regimental administration took place at the mobilization station, which might house a reserve battalion cadre and was responsible for the forward movement of replacements, liaison, and records. A regiment's organization generally contained, both in peacetime and for the greater part of the First World War, three or four battalions, each of which had four companies; a company was further divided into four platoons, each with four sections. Besides the infantry companies, by 1914, each regiment possessed several machine gun sections. An infantry regiment at its full wartime strength would thus number close to 4,500 men. The normal establishment for reserve and second-line regiments was smaller than the regular army regiments.

An infantry company would number only 93 soldiers in peacetime, whereas its war strength might reach 250 men. Upon the proclamation of mobilization, each company required 170–200 men to reach its authorized war establishment. To bridge this gap between peacetime and war strength, each regiment's recruiting district called into service those non-active soldiers who had completed their military training and returned to their civilian occupations. Each infantry regiment's headquarters maintained a roster, which carried the names of approximately 12,000–14,000 men eligible for service. This roster divided the manpower pool within the district into three categories: active soldiers already with their units during peacetime, reserves who would bring units to their wartime strength on mobilization, and substitute reserves who would be sent to replace war losses. Upon the proclamation of mobilization, non-active soldiers had twenty-four hours to arrange for their personal affairs and report to an equipment station. At an equipment station, they would receive clothing and equipment. When a unit reached its war strength, it would go to its mobilization station and await movement to the concentration areas on the frontier. In wartime, the mobilization station dispatched replacements, organized into companies or battalions, to join the regiment in the field. Sometimes temporary brigades were formed from replacement battalions.[31]

During peacetime, the regiments of infantry, cavalry, and artillery were grouped together into brigades, divisions, and corps. A division consisted of four infantry regiments, organized into two brigades, joined with artillery, engineer, and communications units, and a detachment of cavalry. At full strength, then, a division numbered about 20,000 men. The corps command played an important role in the peacetime administration of the army. The corps headquarters acted to coordinate the personnel and equipment of the regiments in its area. It shifted surplus men from one unit to make up for shortages in another. Corps headquarters also maintained lists of non-active soldiers who worked in trades useful to the army after mobilization. At the time of mobilization, the corps commands had the responsibility for creating and organizing units that existed only on paper in peacetime but were necessary to the functioning of the army in war. Transport units, for example, provided necessary logistic support for the army on campaign. Personnel and teams of horses worked the specially designed vehicles for the medical, ammunition, and technical trains stored in depots. Like its manpower resources, army officials generally created an elaborate system to conscript horses for service with the army. Horses were periodically classified according to their usefulness to the army. Owners of horses received a record of conscription, giving them a detailed description of the type of war service their horse might do: the artillery and supply train used heavy draft horses, while lighter horses served as pack animals and pulled smaller wagons. After receiving training, cavalry horses went "on leave"—that is, they went to people who could use them as work animals on condition that they were kept in good physical condition. In Austria-Hungary, keepers received cash bonuses for the good care of these animals, and after several years the horse became the property of its keeper free of charge. In 1914, Germany required over 800,000 horses to meet the wartime needs of its forces for transport, cavalry, and artillery.[32] Besides transport units, the corps commands organized on mobilization second-line military formations and replacement units, which did not exist in peacetime. Only when the corps commands could not find the requisite numbers of men, horses, and material from within its own district did it request help from the war ministry.[33]

To provide security against both foreign attack and sabotage while units were deployed to the frontiers, the proclamation of a "Call to Arms" would take place before mobilization. The first day of the call to arms was generally supposed to precede by twenty-four hours the first day of mobilization; in practice the alarm day might be set several days ahead of the first day of mobilization. During peacetime, some units would be kept at higher readiness so that they could immediately respond to the call to arms. Frontier areas controlled units maintained at higher readiness levels. At mobilization, these units would rush forward to provide border security and remain under the command of the corps headquarters in the frontier regions until their own corps commands arrived in the theater of operations. With local police and militia units, custom officials, and frontier patrols, the units designated to move on the call to arms would act as a covering force—in France called the *couverture*—for the rest of the army during deployment. Meanwhile, to prevent any disruption of mobilization and deployment, men from second-line formations would guard bridges, railway lines, communication centers, and other key posts.[34]

Once mobilization had been completed, the movement of units to the frontier could begin. Those units close to the frontier in peacetime could march on foot directly to the theater of operations. Most units, however, used rail transport to move into the deployment area. An infantry regiment at full war strength, for example, required four trains to move to the area of operations. This movement of troop transports to the frontier was called deployment.[35] Unlike the preparations for mobilization, which were handled primarily at the regimental and corps level, the general staff thoroughly centralized work on deployment plans. Strict regulations concerning the handling and custody of deployment plans severely limited the number of individuals who possessed any detailed knowledge about the deployment of the armed forces on the outbreak of war. Deployment was thus a distinct stage, following mobilization, in the transition of an army or navy from its peacetime location to where it could commence military operations.

Creating and updating these deployment plans was the main function of the general staff in peacetime.[36] Within the general staff, the main burden of the work on deployment plans fell on the sections or bureaus dealing with operations, railway movements, supply, and intelligence. Intelligence officers collected information on foreign military developments, such as a potential adversary's order of battle, weapons' characteristics, railroad construction, and the condition of fortresses. Most importantly, with the technical assistance of the railway planners, who studied an adversary's railway network and capability to move troops, intelligence officers would draw up a picture of the probable deployment areas of the potential enemy army.

With this intelligence assessment in mind, the operations planners created a strategy of campaign that provided the best chances of defeating an enemy's forces. Operations planners formed a high priesthood that decided doctrine. All matters dealing with the "operational art"—that is, the movement and employment of troops on campaign—came within its purview: the organization and evolution of the fighting forces, proposals on fortifications, service regulations for the employment of forces in the field, tactical instructions for field exercises, and the movements of units in the operations area. It also fell to the operations planners to adjudicate the competing military requirements of the various fronts by deciding what forces to deploy against particular potential enemies. Operations planners thus formed the innermost nerve center of "the brains of the army."

In forming their plans, operations planners depended on the railway technicians and supply officers to arrange the transport and logistic support required to carry out the campaign plan. It was the responsibility of the railway planners to develop the detailed transportation plans needed to move these forces at the outbreak of war. In Germany, the general staff's military transport plan called for the movement of over 3,000,000 men and 600,000 horses in 11,000 trains within 13 days. A single bridge over the Rhine at Cologne had to carry 2,150 trains of fifty-four cars each at ten-minute intervals over a seventeen-day period. Each day 650 trains would carry mobilized German forces to their deployment areas on the frontiers with Belgium and France.[37] The railway section thus played an important role alongside the operations planners in all strategic discussions.

Speed of deployment was essential if an army hoped to seize the initiative at the outset of war. Yet the detailed strategies of the railway planners required speed of deployment that might rob the operations officers of the very flexibility they sought in conducting operations. Railway planners understood, and tried to arrive at solutions, to this problem. One staff officer of Austria-Hungary's Railway Bureau saw the problem this way:

[Detailed deployment plans] concealed a grave danger. It was very well realized that events could happen differently, that changes in foreign policy could compel the military leaders to set the army and the military transport system tasks entirely different from those that had been prepared. Deliberations again and again about how these two partly opposed tendencies could be reconciled: on one hand, to make plans as thoroughgoing as possible to obtain a maximum of speed to enable the higher commands a basis for their first efforts; on the other hand, to be ready to fulfill the fundamental duty of the field railways, namely "to satisfy all demands of the leaders at any time." . . . It remained to be seen, however, whether the system, which evolved during many years of work, gave "freedom of decision" to our leaders, and whether it made possible the mastery of the deployment problem as presented by stern reality.[38]

During the July Crisis, this tension between the speed to deploy and flexibility in deployment would surface and pose awkward strategic dilemmas for decision makers.

NOTES

1. The best general accounts on war planning before 1914 are L. L. Farrar, *The Short-War Illusion* (Oxford: Oxford University Press, 1973); and Paul Kennedy, ed., *The War Plans of the Great Powers, 1880–1914* (London: George Allen and Unwin, 1979).

2. Lord Kitchener, who became Britain's secretary of war after the outbreak of fighting, is often pointed to as an example of someone who envisioned a protracted conflict. While it does indeed appear that Kitchener did not think the opening battles would be decisive, his comments about the war's length are so cryptic that it is difficult to know precisely how long he thought the conflict would last. Nonetheless, he remains the exception. See David French, *British Economic and Strategic Planning, 1905–1915* (London: Allen and Unwin, 1982), for an assessment of British views about the war's duration.

3. For a classic statement of this thesis, see Norman Angell, *The Great Illusion: A Study of the Relation of Military Power in Nations to their Economic and Social Advantage* (New York: G. P. Putnam's Sons, 1911). Despite two world wars, this thesis remains popular. See, for example, a recent restatement of it in John Mueller, *Retreat From Doomsday: The Obsolescence of Major War* (New York: Basic Books, 1989).

4. On war as a catalyst for revolution, see Bruce D. Porter, *War and the Rise of the State: The Military Foundations of Modern Politics* (New York: The Free Press, 1994), 15–17.

5. A.J.P. Taylor, *The Struggle for Mastery in Europe, 1848–1914* (Oxford: Oxford University Press, 1971), xxiv.

6. On the importance of the "battle of annihilation" in German military thought, see Jehuda L. Wallach, *The Dogma of the Battle of Annihilation: The Theories*

of Clausewitz and Schlieffen and Their Impact on the German Conduct of Two World Wars (Westport, Conn.: Greenwood Press, 1986).

7. Carl von Clausewitz, *On War*, ed. and trans. Michael Howard and Peter Paret (Princeton: Princeton University Press, 1987), 230–35.

8. On Austria-Hungary's war economy, see Eduard März, *Austrian Banking and Financial Policy: Creditanstalt at a Turning Point, 1913–1923*, trans. Charles Kessler (London: Weidenfeld and Nicolson, 1984), 111–317.

9. The best account of the military operations of the Franco-Prussian War is Michael Howard, *The Franco-Prussian War* (London: Methuen, 1961); and, on the relative economic positions of France and Germany, see Fritz Stern, *Gold and Iron: Bismarck, Bleichröder, and the Building of the German Empire* (New York: Knopf, 1977).

10. März, *Austrian Banking*, 104.

11. Gerhard Ritter, *The Sword and the Scepter*, vol. 2, *The European Powers and the Wilhelmine Empire* (Miami, Fla.: University of Miami Press, 1970); and Gerhard Ritter, *The Schlieffen Plan: Critique of a Myth* (Westport, Conn.: Greenwood Press, 1979).

12. Winston S. Churchill, *The World Crisis*, vol. 6; *The Unknown War* (New York: Charles Scribner's Sons, 1931), 148.

13. Bernard Brodie, *Strategy in the Missile Age* (Princeton: Princeton University Press, 1971), 52.

14. On French military planning before 1914, see Douglas Porch, *The March to the Marne: The French Army, 1871–1914* (Cambridge: Cambridge University Press, 1981); Joel A. Setzen, "The Doctrine of the Offensive in the French Army on the Eve of World War I" (Ph.D. diss., University of Chicago, 1972); Jack Snyder, *The Ideology of the Offensive: Military Decision Making and the Disasters of 1914* (Ithaca, N.Y.: Cornell University Press, 1984), 41–106.

15. Thomas S. Kuhn, *The Structure of Scientific Revolutions*, 2d ed. (Chicago: University of Chicago Press, 1970), 8.

16. Hajo Holborn, "Moltke and Schlieffen: The Prussian-German School," in *Makers of Modern Strategy*, ed. Edward Mead Earle (Princeton: Princeton University Press, 1971), 172–86.

17. Gordon A. Craig, "Delbrück: The Military Historian," in *Makers of Modern Strategy*, 260–83; also see the excellent description of the contrast between the strategy of annihilation and strategy of attrition contained in Raymond Aron, *Clausewitz: Philosopher of War*, trans. Christine Booker and Norman Stone (London: Routledge and Kegan Paul, 1983), 241–64.

18. I. S. Bloch, *The Future of War in Its Technical, Economic and Political Relations: Is War Now Impossible?* (New York: Doubleday and McClure, 1899).

19. Ibid., vii-lxi.

20. Roger Chickering, *Imperial Germany and a World Without War: The Peace Movement and German Society, 1892–1914* (Princeton: Princeton University Press, 1975), 403–5.

21. Geiss, *July 1914*, 47. Sir Edward Grey, Britain's foreign secretary, harbored similar thoughts.

22. Holborn, "Moltke and Schlieffen," 186–205. In addition, on Schlieffen's thinking about war, see Gunther E. Rothenberg, "Moltke, Schlieffen, and the Doctrine of Strategic Envelopment," in *Makers of Modern Strategy*, ed. Peter Paret (Princeton: Princeton University Press, 1986), 296–325.

23. See Michael Howard, "Men against Fire: The Doctrine of the Offensive in 1914," in *Makers of Modern Strategy*, ed. Peter Paret (Princeton: Princeton University Press, 1986), 510–26.

24. See the excellent study by William C. Fuller, Jr., *Strategy and Power in Russia, 1600–1914* (New York: The Free Press, 1992), 394–451. In addition, see Norman Stone, *The Eastern Front, 1914–1917* (New York: Charles Scribner's Sons, 1975), 37–91; and Jack Snyder, *Ideology of the Offensive: Military Decision Making and the Disasters of 1914* (Ithaca, N.Y.: Cornell University Press, 1984), 157–98.

25. Porch, *March to the Marne*; Setzen, "Doctrine of the Offensive"; and Snyder, *Ideology of the Offensive*.

26. Stone, *Eastern Front*, 70–91; and Norman Stone, "Die Mobilmachung der österreichisch-ungarischen Armee 1914," *Militärgeschichtliche Mitteilungen*, 2 (1974): 67–95.

27. Ritter, *Schlieffen Plan*.

28. These developments were foreshadowed by the American Civil War. The general staffs of the European great powers largely ignored the lessons of that conflict. Instead, they focused their attention to the wars of the elder Moltke. On European study of the American Civil War, see Jay Luvaas, *The Military Legacy of the Civil War* (Chicago: University of Chicago Press, 1959), 14–202.

29. Ferdinand Käs, "Versuch einer zusammengefassten Darstellung der Tätigkeit des österreichisch-ungarischen Generalstabes in der Zeit von 1906 bis 1914 unter besonderer Berücksichtung der Aufmarschplanungen und Mobilmachungen" (Ph.D. diss., University of Vienna, 1962), 67–91.

30. Karl Glückmann, *Das Heerwesen der österreichisch-ungarischen Monarchie* (Vienna: Seidel und Sohn, 1911).

31. Oskar Regele, *Feldmarschall Conrad: Auftrag und Erfüllung, 1906–1918* (Vienna: Herold Verlag, 1955) 165–75; Ratzenhofer MSS, 84–91; and Käs, "Generalstabes," 67–98.

32. Arden Bucholz, *Moltke, Schlieffen and Prussian War Planning*, (New York: Berg, 1991), 162.

33. Ratzenhofer MSS, 84–91.

34. Ibid. 78–93; Käs, "Generalstabes," 103–6; *ÖULK*, i, 88.

35. I have chosen to use "deployment" for the German words *Aufmarsch* and *Versammlung*, instead of the more common rendering of "concentration." It is useful to distinguish between deployment—that is, the pre-war planning and initial movements of an army to the frontiers—and concentration, which implies the massing of military formations within an operational theater during the course of a campaign.

36. A distinction was drawn between "concrete war planning" and so-called general war preparations (*allgemeinen Kriegsvorsorgen*), which were concerned with creating and maintaining the Monarchy's war potential (such as organization, equipment, mobilization capabilities, and morale), and not with the deployment and campaign plans directed against a specific adversary. See Käs, "Generalstabes," 29–30; and *AMD*, i, 361–62. In effect, this distinction reflects the difference, outlined by Clausewitz, between "the craft of the swordsmith to the art of fencing." See Clausewitz, *On War*, 133.

37. Bucholz, *Moltke, Schlieffen*, 278.

38. Ratzenhofer MSS, 149–50.

Chapter 2

Austria-Hungary's War Plans

An examination of Austria-Hungary's prewar planning must pay close attention to the strategic ideas, institutional setting, and personality of the chief of the general staff, Baron Franz Conrad von Hötzendorf. The position of chief of the general staff was the most important military post in the Habsburg Monarchy, although nominally it remained only a "helping organ of the War Minister." To use the analogy frequently drawn at the time, the general staff in Vienna was the "brain" of the army. Staff officers on duty with units throughout the Monarchy formed the nervous system, enabling the army to act as a coordinated whole.

That the general staff developed into the most important planning and command authority in the Monarchy was largely due to Baron Friedrich Beck-Rzikowsky. During his long term of service as chief of the general staff—a period lasting twenty-five years—Beck maintained such a close personal relationship with the Kaiser Franz Joseph that he acquired the sobriquet *"Vizekaiser."* Beck worked patiently and tactfully to achieve a premier position for the chief of the general staff in determining the Monarchy's military policy and war plans. By gaining the Kaiser's confidence, he undermined possible centers of bureaucratic opposition, such as the War Minister, the Kaiser's personal military chancellory, or the position of army high command. Beck also achieved success by carefully avoiding any personal or bureaucratic feuds with potential rivals, like the powerful Archduke Albrecht, the victor of Custozza, who held the post of commander-in-chief. In the last analysis, however, the influence of the general staff on the making of military policy depended on the character and personality of its chief.[1]

Under a less bureaucratically skillful or dynamic leader, the general staff's premier position in setting military policy could quickly erode. For example, during General Blasius Schemua's brief tenure of office in 1911–

1912, the chief of staff did not have the same political decision making clout as Beck or Conrad enjoyed during either of their terms in that office. Although not the "zero" that Gerhard Ritter called him,[2] Schemua failed to uphold the position of chief of the general staff. Instead, during Schemua's period as chief, the leadership of the army passed to the far more dynamic war minister, General Moritz von Auffenberg. Conrad, on the other hand, showed the danger of the other extreme of antagonizing other parts of the government or military administration. The rancorous feud between Conrad and the foreign minister Count Alois Aehrenthal resulted in the firing of Conrad from his post as chief of staff in December 1911. Moreover, after 1913 Conrad faced a serious challenge to his position from several quarters within the army establishment. In Bosnia, General Oskar Potiorek managed to gain a large measure of autonomy in his conduct of military operations. His position as governor of the provinces Bosnia-Herzegovina and his influence at court conferred considerable authority on Potiorek in Habsburg policy making. The most serious challenge, however, emanated from the heir apparent Franz Ferdinand, who held the newly created and wide-ranging post of inspector general of the combined armed forces. It is quite clear that, if the assassination of Franz Ferdinand had not occurred, the heir apparent intended to relieve Conrad as chief of staff. Despite the friction engendered by his forceful personality, Conrad exercised extensive powers during his tenure as chief of staff.

As in the other great powers, the general staff in the Habsburg Monarchy was also the center of strategic orthodoxy. The tenets of the short war dogma pervaded the strategic planning of general staff officers. One staff officer recalled: "Before the World War the opinion prevailed that modern wars in Europe would have to be short and that the initial decisions were bound to be especially important. Special attention was therefore attached to a rapid mobilization and surprise deployment of troops in the theater of military operations. . . . The spirit and training of the armed forces and all plans were based primarily on this idea."[3] Another staff officer, who served as an instructor at the War College, remembered how little attention was given to studying recent wars that did not conform to the short war paradigm: "No lectures had as yet been given [by 1914] in the War College on the Russo-Japanese War, since the necessary written material was still lacking. The peculiar features of the Boer War were barely mentioned."[4] Conrad and the staff officers around him believed in the prevalent strategic dogma that a military solution could be reached within the span of a single campaign. Because it did not fit the short war paradigm, any evidence that suggested the next war might last longer than a few months was labeled "peculiar" and "barely mentioned."

In Austria-Hungary, the short war paradigm received further impetus from Conrad's political conception for arresting the decline of the Monarchy. Conrad wanted to wage short, limited wars against the irredentist states of Italy and Serbia. By crippling the military power of these states, he hoped to remove the most serious nationalist and territorial threats to the Monarchy's security. In Conrad's mind, the task of the Monarchy's decision makers was to create the diplomatic and domestic political conditions for these wars to secure the Monarchy's southern frontiers.

In addition, the Monarchy's precarious diplomatic position made it likely that in a future war Austria-Hungary would face a coalition of encircling powers. This coalition would possess a crushing superiority in numbers if it launched a concerted attack. To forestall this possibility, Habsburg military planners would break the encirclement by seizing the initiative and taking the offensive at the onset of war. This action would also protect the Monarchy's territory by taking the fighting onto the enemy's territory. One staff officer remembered: "It thus appeared that the only possibility for a successful outcome in such a desperate situation, was to attack first, hard, and in force at the outset, in the hope of warding off an enemy before he could complete his deployment or before others could join him."[5] Conrad wanted to attack the Monarchy's enemies, by carrying out preemptive strikes in a succession of short wars, before they had a chance to unite. This strategic conception motivated Conrad's constant calls on the foreign ministry first to isolate diplomatically the Monarchy's rivals, and then provoke them into a military contest.

The dogma of the offensive also dominated the prewar thinking on tactics. Before he became chief of the general staff, Conrad had already achieved a reputation throughout the army for his writings on infantry tactics. In these studies, Conrad tried to show that a well-trained infantry could bring decisive success on the battlefield by taking the offensive. Although Conrad recognized the difficulties facing an attacking infantry force because of the increases in firepower available to the defender, he thought that an attacking infantry could keep casualties low by exploiting the advantage of the terrain and by advancing in small columns. At approximately 1,000 yards from enemy positions, the attacking infantry would form a firing line, or a swarm line, and try to gain fire superiority over the defenders. Reinforcements continually fed into the swarm line would replace losses to the attackers. During this phase of the combat, the firing line would also close to within 600 yards of the defender's positions. When it looked as if the attackers had gained fire superiority, the decisive moment of the attack had arrived: fresh infantry, held in reserve away from the fire fight, would reinforce the swarm line to storm the enemy positions and fight (if necessary) with the bayonet. To be successful in its final assault, the infantry must attack with what Conrad called the "categorical imperative to go forward and come to grips with the enemy."[6] The attacker's superiority in morale would bring victory. With well-trained and aggressively led infantry, Conrad believed the attacker would crack the defense.

Once he became chief of the general staff, Conrad sought to make his views on tactics the official army doctrine by having it codified in the service regulations. One contemporary officer called the new service regulations for the infantry, issued in 1911, a "compendium of Conrad's tactics." A more recent military historian agrees, labeling them "Conrad's regulations" because his "spirit" predominated.[7] As in Conrad's earlier writings on tactics, this infantry regulation stressed the advantages of the offensive and the importance of morale: "The offensive, motivated by . . . the thought 'Forward onto the Enemy,' alone can bring decisive success."[8] The new regulations even went to the extreme of saying morale was more important than superiority in numbers: one section stated that attacking infantry, "without the support of other arms, even in inferior numbers, [can] gain victory as long as it is tough and brave."[9] Only the French army, which had embraced the teachings of the *offensive à outrance* school, entered the First World War as insistent on the superiority of the offensive. One staff officer recalled: "The k.u.k. Army, and all other organizations of the Empire which were at its disposal, were therefore organized, equipped, and trained for an offensive war."[10]

Of course, the reality of combat would show the dangers of this offensive conception of warfare. Conrad bears the primary responsibility for the growth of a tactical doctrine that extolled the supremacy of morale and the offensive over numbers, material, and the defense. Conrad promoted a mismatch between doctrine and the capabilities of modern weapons. Austria-Hungary, as well as France, would pay a heavy price in 1914 for this lopsided reliance on the offensive.

Upon taking over as chief of staff, Conrad thoroughly immersed himself in the drafting of war plans. Conrad saw this task as his primary responsibility and took a special interest in it. In his memoirs, Conrad continued to look upon war planning as the central function of the general staff: "The most important task of the general staff, in peacetime, and the most responsible duty of the chief of the general staff, is concerned with the so-called concrete war plans."[11] The officers on the general staff quickly noticed Conrad's determination to provide impetus and direction to war planning: "From the very beginning he [Conrad] considered his most important duty—as his predecessor had done—to be the planning and organization of concrete war plans, to which he immediately devoted his enormous capacity for work."[11] Conrad worked closely with the chief of the Operations Bureau of the general staff. In 1910, this Bureau was led by Lieutenant-Colonel Josef Metzger. Conrad thought the selection of Metzger as Chief of the Operations Bureau a "fortunate choice." In his memoirs, Conrad praised Metzger for his "clear vision of the great questions [and] full control of the details." The two men worked closely together in drafting operational plans.[13]

Interestingly, one of his first decisions was to stop war planning against Austria-Hungary's ally Germany. Until Conrad's arrival, Habsburg military planners had continued to draw up as part of their annual planning exercises a war plan against Germany. Conrad did not need a plan of campaign against Germany because his attention was drawn to providing for the security of the Monarchy's southern frontiers. Thus, he imparted great energy to the development of war plans against Italy and Serbia. That Conrad focused Habsburg war planning on Italy and Serbia is surprising, since Russia was clearly the Monarchy's most formidable potential great-power adversary. Conrad was obsessed, however, with striking down those states that possessed an irredentist claim against the Monarchy. Moreover, while Russia's military power remained paralyzed by defeat and domestic unrest in the aftermath of the Russo-Japanese War, Conrad thought the Monarchy possessed a window of opportunity to attack its southern neighbors. Another factor was Conrad's realistic assessment that the Monarchy had the military strength only to defeat Serbia and Italy.

The most difficult strategic problem confronting operations planners in Austria-Hungary was the way to apportion the army's fighting forces at the beginning of war. Austria-Hungary lacked the military resources to carry out a "one-and-a-half war" strategy, where the forces fight a major conflict against another great power while simultaneously conducting operations against a smaller state on another front. Russia by itself outclassed Austria-Hungary in military power.

While Conrad was certain that the Monarchy had to face Serbia in any future war, he could not be sure of his major antagonist. Before 1912, he saw an irredentist Italy as the most dangerous great-power rival facing Austria-Hungary. After that date, Conrad felt Russia posed the most serious threat. The large-scale Russian army maneuvers along the Monarchy's frontiers, undertaken to support client states in the Balkan Wars, showed in a heavy-handed manner the recovery of Tsarist military power from the twin shocks of the defeat in the Far East and the subsequent internal upheaval. After the Balkan Wars, Romania also emerged as a possible future enemy.

Austria-Hungary's strategic position had become desperate: it could not hope to compete in armaments with the combination of Russia, Italy, Serbia, and Romania. Consequently, operations planners worked at devising schemes for dealing with the various possible military contingencies. Operations planners did not base their strategy on a "worst case" scenario, namely that of war with a coalition of Russia, Italy, Serbia, and Romania. Although the First World War would show such a coalition was not unrealistic, this scenario was too far beyond the military forces available to the Monarchy. Operations planners counted on the diplomacy of the Ballhausplatz to prevent the formation of an overwhelming combination of enemy states.

The most important premise behind deployment plans was that Austria-Hungary would face only one great power rival at a time. Yet the general staff could not predict with certainty the Monarchy's diplomatic position when war became inevitable. Unlike their German counterparts, who after 1913 came to rely on only the Schlieffen Plan in case of war, Habsburg military planners updated several deployment plans in an attempt to keep abreast of the changing diplomatic situation facing Austria-Hungary. They sought to accomplish this by dividing the army's combat formations into three groups and devising flexible transportation schemes to move them to the frontiers in a crisis. With the proclamation of mobilization, formations became available for movement to the theater of operations according to a schedule. Because of the decentralized peacetime administration of the army, policy makers in the Habsburg Monarchy possessed some flexibility in carrying out mobilization. Army Manual J-1, entitled "Mobilization Instructions," lists the alternate methods for mobilization. General mobilization would occur in case of war with another great power, such as Italy and Russia. The general staff also wrote plans for partial mobilization, in which only a portion of the Monarchy's military units came up to war strength. Partial mobilization would provide the Monarchy with the military strength it required to undertake a military campaign into the Balkans, if other great powers—such as Russia or Italy—refrained from interfering. The general staff also developed plans for the independent mobilization of individual corps areas, select formations (such as cavalry units), and the movement of units from their territorial areas without first bringing them up to war strength by calling up non-active soldiers. These mobilization options gave the Monarchy's decision makers a considerable degree of flexibility in calling up military forces. The Monarchy used all these mobilization options to support its foreign policy during the period between the Bosnian Crisis and the outbreak of war in 1914.[14]

The *"Minimalgruppe Balkan"* consisted primarily of three army corps (eight divisions) located in Croatia, Bosnia, and Dalmatia in peacetime: XIII Corps with its headquarters located in Agram, XV Corps headquartered in Sarajevo, and XVI Corps in Ragusa.[15] The primary mission of these forces was to guard against a Serbian attack and protect the southern frontier of the Monarchy. When the *Minimalgruppe Balkan* completed deployment in northeastern Bosnia, it could directly defend Sarajevo and threaten the flank of any Serbian advance toward Budapest.[16] A system of fortifications and blockhouses made a Serbian invasion of Bosnia very difficult. Because of the hostility between Belgrade and Vienna, Habsburg military planners expected Serbia to attack Austria-Hungary if the latter became embroiled in a war with Russia or Italy. The wartime strength of the Serbian army was greater than the *Minimalgruppe Balkan*. Consequently, its three corps were to stand on the defensive at the outbreak of a war between the Habsburg Monarchy and Russia or Italy. This deployment scheme and defensive operations plan was code colored Plan Brown. Only after the defeat of Russia or Italy, when more forces became available, would an offensive begin against Serbia.

The remaining thirteen corps of the Habsburg army were divided into two further groups: the *"A"-Staffel* consisting of nine corps and the *"B"-Staffel* of four corps. In a war with either Russia or Italy, the *"A"-Staffel* would deploy to the main theater of operations, followed closely by the *"B"-Staffel*. Once deployed, these two groups of thirteen corps would begin an offensive across the frontiers. Habsburg operational doctrine stressed the value of paralyzing the military actions of an adversary by taking the offensive and obtaining the initiative at the outset of a campaign. One operational manual instructed field commanders: "It is important, at the beginning of the campaign, to seize the initiative to oneself by relentless, offensive, forward movements, and thereby maintain it throughout the entire campaign."[17]

Habsburg military planners also prepared for a conflict that remained limited (at least initially) to only Austria-Hungary and Serbia. Once a war with Serbia started, however, Habsburg planners feared that the conflict would not remain confined to the Balkans. Habsburg planners estimated that Russia or Italy would seize the opportunity offered by a Balkan war to intervene on the side of Serbia against the Monarchy. It seemed imperative, then, that Habsburg forces attack at once in an attempt to destroy the Serbian army and overrun the kingdom of Serbia in a quick campaign. To carry out this offensive, the four corps of the *"B"-Staffel* would reinforce the three corps of the *Minimalgruppe Balkan*. Only by deploying seven corps, organized in three armies, were Habsburg military planners confident of rapidly defeating Serbia in a localized war before Russia or Italy could intervene. By undertaking a concentric attack across the Sava and Drina rivers, the three Habsburg armies aimed at bringing the Serbian army to battle and encircling it along the Bosnian frontier. Once this battle along the frontier was completed, the Habsburg armies would advance into the center of the Serbian kingdom, capturing Belgrade along the way. In the campaign against Serbia, the so-called Danube flotilla, armored gunboats, would bombard Serbian positions and guard against an invasion of Hungary. Labeled Case B for Balkan and code-named Plan Yellow (to distinguish it from the defensive Plan Brown), this plan called for a rapid victory over Serbia by a major offensive effort.

While the attack against Serbia called for in Plan Yellow progressed, some of the corps comprising the *"A"-Staffel* would stand ready for deployment to Galicia or the Italian frontier in case Russia or Italy entered the conflict. The III Corps with its headquarters in Graz and the XIV Corps in the Tyrol would protect the Monarchy's frontiers against an Italian military intervention; meanwhile, the I, X, and XI corps in Galicia would guard against a Russian attack. The general staff also drew up plans to transfer forces fighting against Serbia to the Russian or Italian frontiers in an emergency.[18]

The most important strategic decision facing Habsburg policy makers at the outset of war involved the deployment the *"B"-Staffel*. The Serbian frontier required the deployment of the *Minimalgruppe Balkan*, and the *"A"-Staffel* would provide security against either Russia or Italy. The *"B"-Staffel*, however, could deploy to whatever front the Monarchy's decision makers deemed most critical. This force was essential for the success of any opening offensives. In the Balkans, the *"B"-Staffel* provided military superiority over Serbia. Meanwhile, most of the war plans against Russia or Italy required its timely arrival in the theater of operations.

Planning for war against Italy was of special interest to Conrad. Before assuming the position of chief of the general staff, Conrad had served as commander of various units stationed along the Italian frontier. He had witnessed firsthand the dangers of the Italian irredentist movement in Trieste. As commander of the Eighth Infantry Division in the Tyrol, he also had an opportunity to study closely the problems of fighting Italy in the rugged mountain conditions along the Monarchy's Alpine frontiers. It was Conrad's personal conviction that a war against Italy was inevitable. In a memorandum to Kaiser Franz Joseph written shortly after taking the position of chief of staff, Conrad warned that "Italy is the one [state] with whom conflict is most likely at the present time."[19]

War Plan I for Italy, code-named Red, envisioned an attack by four Habsburg armies across the Italian frontier after the completion of deployment by the twentieth day of mobilization.[20] Three of these armies, totaling more than twenty-six infantry divisions, would spearhead the offensive, attacking along the Isonzo front from Trieste at the head of the Adriatic to Mauthern in the Carinthian Alps. Assisting this main offensive, a fourth army deployed in the Tyrol would strike down the Brenta River valley toward Padua. This army's goal was to sever the lines of communication of the Italian forces in Venetia facing the Isonzo front. Habsburg military planners thought that the high trajectory Skoda 305–cm artillery mortars would play an especially useful role in reducing Italian fortresses in the way of their offensive.

The Habsburg general staff realized that a war between the Monarchy and Italy might widen to include other states, such as Serbia and Montenegro. Consequently, contingency plans were also drawn up by Habsburg planners in case the Monarchy became embroiled in a conflict with Serbia and Montenegro at the same time they fought Italy. More troubling to Habsburg planners was the contingency posed by a hostile Russia threatening intervention during a conflict between Austria-Hungary and Italy. In both these last cases, the number of divisions deployed against Italy would be scaled back to provide forces for the security of the Monarchy's Balkan and Galician frontiers. One staff study, for instance, considered the contingency where the I, X, and XI corps in Galicia were withheld from the Italian front. Instead, they would provide a strategic *couverture* for the Monarchy against a Russian attack. While perhaps as many as twelve divisions might be drawn away for these security duties, Habsburg war plans still envisioned taking the offensive across the Isonzo against Italy. Despite the high risk of taking the offensive, Habsburg planners nonetheless thought that the rapid defeat of Italy provided the best strategic alternative. They also confidently maintained that their forces could quickly overrun northern Italy and destroy the main troop concentrations of the Italian army within the span of a single campaign.

Planning for war against Russia, on the other hand, haunted Habsburg staff officers because a Russian campaign seemed simply beyond the military resources of the Monarchy. Further, there appeared no way to defeat Russia in a rapid campaign. "Of all the possibilities of war," Conrad confessed, "it is the Russian that I look forward to with the greatest anxiety and I desire that it not begin." Oskar Regele has observed: "In this wish, the chief of the general staff was of a mind with the Heir Apparent [Franz Ferdinand], who also saw a war with Russia as an eventuality to be avoided."[21] The recovery of Russian military power, however, forced the Monarchy's military leaders to face a new grim strategic reality. After the Balkan Wars, they needed to focus their attention on planning for a two-front war with Russia and Serbia.

Of course, Conrad could not neglect planning for war against Russia, even though his main interest was in developing deployment and operational plans for attacking Italy or Serbia. Throughout the nineteenth century Habsburg planners had studied the strategic problems of waging a war against Russia. A corps of 45,000 Austrian soldiers, commanded by Count Karl von Schwarzenberg, fought on Napoleon's side during the famous 1812 campaign in Russia. Schwarzenberg's corps, initially concentrated at Lemberg, marched into Russia on the right flank of Napoleon's *Grande Armée*. The Austrian force fought several battles against the Russians in the western Ukraine. At the time of the Crimean War, the Austrian general staff drew up a plan for an Austro-Prussian campaign against Russia. This plan called for concentrating the main body of the Austrian army in eastern Galicia and an advance into Russian Poland. At the time of the great Near Eastern Crisis of 1877–1878, the general staff, headed by Baron Anton Schönfeld and his chief deputy Beck, also drew up plans for a war against Russia.[22]

It was only in 1881, however, with the appointment of Beck as chief of the general staff, that Habsburg war planning against Russia took on a more systematic character. The essence of Beck's early plans was to take advantage of Austria-Hungary's superior railway facilities to concentrate a force of three armies (approximately twenty-six divisions) in Galicia and take the offensive into Poland before Russia's forces were fully prepared. Beck intended "to destroy the Russians during their period of concentration."[23] Two armies would attack northward between the Vistula and Bug rivers, while a third army provided flank protection from a Russian advance from the Ukraine. Habsburg planners considered it essential that this third army join in the northern offensive. By attacking toward Rovno, this army would both tie down Russian forces in the region and disrupt the Russian railway network. A massive raid by Habsburg cavalry units, designed to disrupt the Russian deployment, would precede the general offensive. Habsburg planners also counted on Romania's participation as an ally tying down Russian forces in Bessarabia.

Conrad agreed with and followed the general outline developed by Beck. His main change in the operational plan was to distribute the Habsburg forces deployed in Galicia among four armies rather than three. As in Beck's plan, three armies would attack into Russian Poland from their deployment areas around Przemsyl and Lemberg. The remaining army—the Second Army under Conrad's scheme—was to take up a covering position along the Sereth River between Tarnopol and Czernowitz. Its assigned objective was to protect the eastern flank of the northern offensive.

In his early operational plans, drawn up during the Bosnian Crisis, Conrad also counted on a Romanian offensive into Bessarabia to distract an entire Russian army away from Galicia. Later Habsburg war plans, drawn up during and after the Balkan wars, no longer counted on Romania's participation as an ally; instead, planners increasingly viewed Romania as a potential adversary in any war with Russia. But Austria-Hungary could not spare front-line forces to protect this frontier. Consequently, Habsburg planners counted on *Landsturm* units, fighting from fortified positions in the mountain passes along the frontier, to blunt any Romanian offensive during the initial stage of a conflict. When forces became available from the main theater of war in Galicia, Habsburg military leaders intended to mount a campaign to recapture any territory lost to Romania. The outcome of the Balkan wars—in particular, the strengthening of Serbia's military power and the potential defection of Romania as an ally—made the Monarchy's Balkan frontiers far less secure.

On the eve of the First World War, the resurgence of Russian military strength also called into question the viability of Habsburg plans for an offensive into Poland. The most important change in this regard was the improvements made by the Russian empire in upgrading its railway network. These improvements meant that Russia's military deployment would no longer lag behind that of the Monarchy. Consequently, Habsburg forces could no longer count on possessing a superior force during the initial stage of a conflict. By 1914 Habsburg planners, relying on good intelligence on Russian developments, calculated that Russia could already deploy its forces along the Galician border faster than could the Monarchy. Russian forces could undertake their own early offensive, before the Habsburg deployment was complete. Furthermore, the military situation against Russia would only grow worse. By 1917, when Russia would complete its military expansion and railway improvement programs, the

Russian army could deploy eighty infantry divisions against Germany and Austria-Hungary only eighteen days after the declaration of mobilization. Since Germany and Austria-Hungary expected to deploy only about fifty divisions on their eastern borders, Russia would possess a substantial measure of superiority in the initial battles. The Central Powers thus faced the necessity of revising their deployment plans and reinforcing the armies fighting Russia.[24]

Another factor disturbing to Conrad was that because of the treason of Colonel Alfred Redl, Russian intelligence had a great deal of information about Habsburg deployment plans. Redl provided his Russian handlers with considerable information about Austrian fortresses in Galicia and deployment plans of Habsburg forces.[25] This treason forced Habsburg planners to undertake major revisions in their plans.

Because of Russia's growing military prowess, Conrad ordered that staff planners begin considering the option of deploying Habsburg forces further back from the frontier. Habsburg planners considered countering the increasingly rapid pace of Russia's deployment by evacuating most of eastern Galicia at the outset of a war. Of course, this course also meant the abandonment of any early offensive by Austria-Hungary. Conrad's interest in deploying away from the frontiers had important consequences for the conduct of the initial campaign of the war.

While Habsburg staff planners were revising their assessment of the military balance with Russia, the official plan remained that of an early attack into Russian Poland. Although he increasingly doubted the feasibility of an early offensive against Russia, Conrad did not abandon the attack plan that had formed the basis for over thirty years of Habsburg strategic planning. Conrad summed up his thinking about the military situation facing the Monarchy by saying that he "planned an early offensive." Thus, prewar military planning in Austria-Hungary contained a strong bias in favor of offensive operations. It is hardly surprising, then, to see Habsburg armies taking the offensive in the opening round of the war in an attempt to deliver a knockout blow. By extolling the virtues of the offensive, and discounting more sober assessments of the relative balance of forces, Conrad deserves much of the blame for the heavy defeats suffered by the Habsburg army during the war's opening battles.

NOTES

1. On Austria-Hungary's war planning, see Gunther F. Rothenberg, *The Army of Francis Joseph* (West Lafayette, Ind.: Purdue University Press, 1976), 105–71.

2. Ritter, *Sword and the Scepter*, ii, 231.

3. Ratzenhofer MSS, 97.

4. de Bartha, "The Austro-Hungarian General Staff," unpublished manuscript, dated August 1946, trans. J. B. Robinson, U.S. Army Military History Research Collection, Carlisle Barracks, Pa., 42.

5. Ratzenhofer MSS, 97.

6. Franz Conrad von Hötzendorf, *Die Gefectsausbildung der,* 4th ed. *Infanterie* (Vienna: Verlag von L. W. Seidel und Sohn, 1907), 216. This book went through a total of five editions between 1900 and the outbreak of war.

7. Colonel Rudolf Rudel, *Streffleurs Militärische Zeitschrift,* 1 (1912), 412; Oskar Regele, *Feldmarschall Conrad,* 207; Rothenberg, *Army of Francis Joseph,* 143.

8. Regele, *Feldmarschall Conrad,* 208.

9. Quoted in Rothenberg, *Army of Francis Joseph,* 143.

10. Ratzenhofer MSS, 97.

11. *AMD,* i, 361.

12. Ratzenhofer MSS, 27.

13. *AMD,* i, 363–66; ii, 51; iii, 604.

14. Käs, "Generalstabes," 101–2.

15. Stone, "Mobilmachung," provides details of the peacetime location of corps areas.

16. The general staff's deployment and operations plans against Serbia can be found in KA, GenStab, OpB, Fasz. 42.

17. Regele, *Feldmarschall Conrad,* 201.

18. Ratzenhofer MSS, 174.

19. *AMD,* i, 509–10.

20. The various war plans drawn up against Italy during Conrad's tenure of office can be found in KA, GenStab, OpB, Fasz. 38–40. In addition, see the study by Hans Jürgen Pantenius, *Der Angriffsgedanke gegen Italien bei Conrad von Hötzendorf* (Vienna: Böhlau, 1983).

21. Regele, *Feldmarschall Conrad,* 49.

22. Edmund von Glaise-Horstenau, *Franz Josephs Weggefährte: Dashebendes Generalstabschefs Grafen Beck* (Vienna: Amalthea Verlag, 1930), 38. The following discussion of early Habsburg war plans against Russia draws heavily on the research of Glaise-Horstenau on Beck's tenure as chief of staff.

23. Max Freiherr von Pitreich, *1914: Die militärischen Probleme unseres Kriegsbeginnes* (Vienna: Selbstverlag, 1934), 19–21.

24. Norman Stone, "Austria-Hungary," *Knowing One's Enemies: Intelligence Assessment Before the Two World Wars,* ed. Ernest R. May (Princeton: Princeton University Press, 1984), 45–46. It should be noted that Russian infantry divisions were larger than their German and Austro-Hungarian counterparts. A Russian division contained sixteen infantry battalions, whereas those of Germany and Austria-Hungary contained only twelve. Thus, the disparity in manpower between Russia and the Central Powers on the eastern front was greater than is indicated by their relative strength in divisions.

25. On the Redl story, see the short accounts by Alan Sked, "A Patriot for Whom?" *History Today,* 36 (1986): 9–15; and Ian D. Armour, "Colonel Redl: Fact and Fantasy," *Intelligence and National Security,* 2, 1 (1987): 170–83. In addition, see the exhaustive study done by Georg Markus, *Der Fall Redl* (Vienna: Amalthea Verlag, 1984). A more entertaining, fictional account of Redl, based on extensive research in the *Kriegsarchiv* in Vienna, is provided by Robert B. Asprey, *The Panther's Feast* (London: Jonathan Cape, 1959).

Chapter 3

Prewar Military Collaboration Between Austria-Hungary and Germany

War planners in Austria-Hungary and Germany before 1914 faced the strategic predicament of being encircled by a numerically superior coalition if war broke out. Although the German and Austro-Hungarian general staffs recognized this strategic problem, they had not prepared any detailed plans to coordinate their military operations. They failed, then, to take advantage of the "interior lines" accorded them by their countries' geographical position in the heart of Europe. This strategic problem interested Ludwig Beck, who served as chief of the German general staff during the 1930s. In an essay written in 1941, Beck argued: "The numerical superiority of the enemy in 1914 required that the German and Austro-Hungarian armies adopt a coordinated plan to exploit their interior lines and to avoid exposing the latter forces to isolation and defeat by superior Russian forces."[1] Instead of developing an operations plan based on these strategic principles, however, the Central Powers launched offensives simultaneously on three fronts: the Germans striking at France, and Habsburg armies attacking on both the Galician and Serbian fronts. Like the Axis powers in the Second World War, the German and Austro-Hungarian general staffs dispersed their military effort in uncoordinated offensives. Consequently, they failed to achieve the short, decisive war they hoped for and, instead, found themselves deadlocked on all fronts in a protracted conflict against a coalition that possessed superior resources.

Lack of detailed operational planning between the two staffs before the war helps to explain how this stalemate occurred. Military collaboration between the Central Powers was essentially limited to conversations and an exchange of letters at the chief of staff level. These talks failed to outline strategic priorities in even general terms, let alone make binding military commitments. The staffs of the Entente powers, on the other hand, drew up detailed plans coordinating their military operations in case of war.[2] The

failure of the Central Powers to elaborate a common military strategy before
the war reflects the divergent political ambitions that were to dog their
relations during the war.

Conrad's underlying political motive was to overcome the Monarchy's
interrelated internal and external problems, which required a successful,
short, limited war. In his view, the irredentist states of Serbia and Italy posed
the most serious threats to the Monarchy's survival as a great power.
Conrad viewed preventive war as the best solution for eliminating these
threats. He argued that the Monarchy must "aim at settling accounts with
its aggressive, inevitable enemies by engaging them separately." This "policy of action" would arrest the Monarchy's decline; war would provide
internal stability. Like Germany's *Weltmachtpolitik*, the policy of action had
no precise timetable for completion, only that the Monarchy must move
quickly to settle accounts with Serbia and Italy before Russia recovered
from its defeat in the Russo-Japanese War of 1904–1905.[3]

An important component of this scheme to revitalize the Monarchy was
the military alliance with Germany. Germany provided, in Conrad's view,
a makeweight against Russia, deterring Russian intervention in Austria-
Hungary's war with Serbia or Italy. Moreover, in case deterrence failed,
Conrad wanted Germany to launch an offensive into Russian Poland to
divert Russia's attention from the Habsburg Monarchy. With Russia's forces
tied down containing a German attack, the Habsburg Monarchy could carry
out its own offensive in the Balkans or on the Italian frontier. Military
planning in Austria-Hungary during Conrad's tenure of office as chief of
staff only makes sense if this perspective on Germany's role is kept in mind.

Berlin and the German general staff, however, had a different outlook on
the importance of military collaboration between Germany and Austria-
Hungary. Germany's leadership looked upon Austria-Hungary's armies as
playing a pivotal role in tying down Russian forces. The German army, then,
could mass most of its strength against France to obtain a knockout blow
in the west during the initial campaign—the famous Schlieffen Plan. These
differing conceptions of the nature of the military collaboration between
Austria-Hungary and Germany would have serious consequences in 1914.
An examination of the prewar military relations between Austria-Hungary
and Germany is very important for understanding the decisions taken in
Berlin and Vienna during the July Crisis. The outcome of the initial campaigns of the First World War also rested on the collaboration between the
two staffs before 1914.

Finally, an analysis of the military collaboration between the two general
staffs can determine whether these discussions changed the fundamental
nature of the 1879 alliance between Austria-Hungary and Germany, turning
it from a strictly defensive arrangement into an offensive pact. This change
in the nature of the alliance between Vienna and Berlin is considered
decisive in causing the outbreak of the First World War. Gordon Craig, for

example, in his widely read study *The Politics of the Prussian Army*, argues that the staff agreements reached by Conrad and Helmuth von Moltke, the chief of the German general staff, "amounted to an admission that Austria had a right to expect German support even in a war caused by her own provocation."[4] In effect, Germany was endorsing a policy of expansion by the Habsburg Monarchy in the Balkans. Close examination of these staff discussions and of the international crises that entangled the Habsburg Monarchy before 1914 does not support Craig's thesis. While the two general staffs did engage in discussions of strategic planning, these talks did not in any fundamental way change the underlying tenets of the alliance between Austria-Hungary and Germany. In confrontations with Russia and Serbia in 1908–1909, 1911–1912, and 1914, Vienna did not count on and did not receive the unconditional support of Berlin despite the existence of these talks. The staff talks between Conrad and Moltke do not betray any concrete, common, long-range plan to wage a preventive war. These talks were even more limited in scope than the military discussions between Britain and France, and between France and Russia.[5] Yet, few historians would argue that, because of those military discussions, Britain, France, and Russia intended to wage a preventive war against Germany and Austria-Hungary in 1914. A detailed examination of the staff talks between Austria-Hungary and Germany makes it possible to assess their impact on the diplomacy of Vienna and Berlin. These talks had little impact in changing the nature of the alliance from a defensive to an offensive orientation.

When the Habsburg Monarchy and Germany first concluded an alliance in 1879, Bismarck envisaged it as part of his pan-European diplomatic system of checks and balances. His diplomacy aimed at keeping France isolated and preventing the encirclement of Germany by a hostile coalition of great powers. An alliance with Austria-Hungary served as a precaution against it becoming a part of any coalition threatening Germany; consequently, it eliminated Bismarck's fear of a revival of the Kaunitz coalition of Austria, France, and Russia that faced Prussia during the Seven Years' War. The alliance also made sense geographically because it removed the prospect of military confrontation along Germany's long frontier with Austria-Hungary. (This frontier was roughly equivalent in length to Germany's borders with France and Russia combined.) Bismarck also saw this alliance as useful in helping to recreate the alignment of Germany, Austria-Hungary, and Russia. This bloc of powers had fallen apart because of the great Near Eastern crisis and the Congress of Berlin. Thus, despite the obvious security advantages that accrued to Germany, Bismarck did not intend the alliance as a military pact aimed at Russia. Instead, he saw it as a strictly limited defensive alliance, designed to give Berlin the diplomatic initiative in relations among the three great eastern monarchies.[6]

The military collaboration between the two countries remained limited in scope, although Bismarck did sanction discussions between the two staffs. In April 1882, the new chief of staff in Austria-Hungary, Friedrich Baron Beck-Rzikowsky, urged the adoption of explicit arrangements for the coordination of the two armies in case of war with Russia. Beck wanted specific commitments from Germany because he was aware of the Habsburg Monarchy's distinct military inferiority in relation to Tsarist Russia. Without German military assistance, Beck concluded that Russia would defeat Austria-Hungary in any conflict between them. The first conversations between the two staffs occurred in August 1882 when Beck met with General Alfred von Waldersee, the quartermaster-general and first assistant to the German chief of staff Field Marshal Helmuth von Moltke, the hero of the German wars of unification. During the next five years Beck and Moltke continued to improve relations between the two general staffs by an exchange of letters. Even during the First World War, when the very survival of the two monarchies depended on close military cooperation, relations between the two staffs were not as intimate as in this period.[7]

This closeness rested in large part on Moltke's strategic views. Moltke believed that, if a general European war occurred, Germany must concentrate considerable forces—perhaps as much as half the German army—in the east against Russia.[8] Furthermore, he planned to carry out an immediate offensive into Russian Poland. Moltke expected France to take advantage of any war between Germany and Russia to avenge Sedan and recover Alsace-Lorraine. Thus, he thought Germany must be prepared to fight a two-front war. In one memorandum on the subject of a two-front war, Moltke wrote: "we should exploit the great advantages that the Rhine and our powerful fortifications confer to the defensive in the west and should employ all the combat forces that are not absolutely needed [against France] for a massive offensive in the east."[9]

Beck could ask for nothing more of his ally than what Moltke offered: Austria-Hungary received assurances of powerful military support in a war with Russia. For his part, Beck committed Habsburg armies to the earliest possible attack from Galicia into Russian Poland. This attack would support Moltke's offensive. The commitment to an early offensive was a prominent feature of Habsburg war plans in case of a conflict with Russia.

The military commitments made by Moltke, however, did not change Bismarck's limited conception of the Dual Alliance: neither monarchy would have found its political freedom of action circumscribed by detailed operational plans, as the military collaboration between the British and French bound those governments in the decade before 1914. Bismarck saw to it that the general staff foreclosed none of his political options: he smashed the 1887 attempts of Beck and Waldersee, during the Bulgarian Crisis, to draw up a detailed military convention, or to change the definition of the casus foederis from a defensive to an offensive alliance. Bismarck thus ensured that military collaboration between the two staffs remained limited to nothing more than an exchange of letters and periodic meetings at the chief-of-staff level. In this way, the two staffs could discuss in only general terms a common military strategy for the two monarchies in case of war.[10]

Even the passing of Bismarck from the political scene did not lead to a greater closeness between Austria-Hungary and Germany. Instead, the opposite occurred. The cordiality in military relations between the two staffs deteriorated with the appointment of Count Alfred von Schlieffen as the German chief of staff in 1891. At their first meeting in April 1891, Beck found the new German chief of staff "taciturn and not very obliging."[11] Perhaps, as Gerhard Ritter has surmised, Schlieffen's abruptness with Beck revealed even at this early date his intention to break from the deployment plans of Moltke and Waldersee and mass the bulk of the German army against France instead of Russia. In a memorandum written in April 1891, Schlieffen contended that the German armies could overcome the French line of fortifications along the Franco-German frontier: "Against this vast force, the French fortifications—since they could be by-passed through Belgium—would not form a great enough obstacle to rule out an offensive."[12] This marked an important change from the strategic planning of Moltke and Waldersee. Schlieffen saw in a gigantic wheeling action by the German armies through Belgium—a *manoeuvres sur les derrières* like that used by Napoleon in the campaigns of Marengo, Ulm, and Jena—a way to destroy France's armies in a single campaign.[13]

The destruction of France's armed forces in a single campaign entailed massing the bulk of the German army in the west. This meant, however, leaving Austria-Hungary alone to face Russia during the initial stage of a two-front war. Until December 1895, Schlieffen continued to discuss with Beck plans for fighting Russia. Schlieffen's intention to defeat France first before massing against Russia resulted in a growing antagonism between the two chiefs. Their emerging antagonism, then, was rooted in their divergent views on the proper strategy to follow.[14] Schlieffen expressed this antagonism in remarks to his aides: "I say we must beat France first; His Excellency [Beck], of course, says that Russia is the main thing." Beck began to complain that he did not receive as much information from Schlieffen as he did from Moltke and Waldersee. Relations between the two men became so strained that Schlieffen dropped further correspondence with Beck early in 1896. Of course, Beck realized that Schlieffen's refusal to reopen relations between the two staffs did not bode well for obtaining German military support in a war with Russia. Although Beck could not be certain that Schlieffen had abandoned earlier German plans to concentrate in the east, he must have suspected it. Instead of dwelling on this dismal prospect, however, Beck continued to plan his offensive from Galicia, counting upon a German offensive into Russia. This atmosphere of uncertainty apparently suited Schlieffen as well, because in January 1896 he wrote: "It is impossible to tell Beck that the emphasis of German operations is now in the West, or he will become even more suspicious."[15] Thus, Schlieffen's attitude toward his ally was that the less told to Beck the better! Within five years of becoming Germany's chief of staff, Schlieffen had broken off relations between the two staffs. Moreover, he intentionally meant to deceive Beck about the shift in German strategy from an offensive against Russia to one against France. After this break in 1896, the two staffs developed their plans independently of one another over the next decade: Beck refined the Habsburg strike from Galicia, while Schlieffen further elaborated his plan against France.

Germany's military planners looked for a way to fight a two-front war. Frederick the Great once wrote that Prussia must fight "short and lively" wars; Prussian generals should seek a speedy decision.[16] Schlieffen, a close student of the wars of Frederick and Napoleon, took this precept to heart. He aimed at nothing less than winning decisively in several short campaigns. To accomplish this aim, he concluded that Germany needed to concentrate against one enemy at a time and leave a minimum of forces on other fronts. This "win-hold-win" strategy rested on exploiting the strategic vulnerabilities of Germany's adversaries. (Frederick had also said that he who defends everything defends nothing.) The Schlieffen plan's main elements deserve close examination.[17]

First, Schlieffen considered it feasible to defeat France quickly. To Schlieffen, France was the most dangerous enemy Germany would have to face; the Russian defeats in Manchuria and subsequent revolutions in 1905 seemed to confirm his analysis. He wrote in one memorandum: "The *whole* of Germany must throw itself on *one* enemy—the strongest, the most dangerous enemy: and that can only be the Anglo-French." Schlieffen would not let entreaties from Vienna dissuade Germany from this plan: "Austria need not worry: the Russian army will not invade Galicia before the die is cast in the West. And Austria's fate will be decided not on the Bug but on the Seine!"[18]

Geography made France a tempting initial target. Paris and important industrial regions of France lie close to the German and Belgian borders. To protect these regions, French forces needed to fight a forward defense. By the early nineteenth century, Clausewitz saw this as a French vulnerability. In many key respects, Clausewitz even outlines the Schlieffen Plan in Book Eight, Chapter Nine of *On War*. Significantly, the chapter is entitled: "The Plan of a War Designed to Lead to the Total Defeat of the Enemy." As Clausewitz noted: "The center of gravity of France lies in the armed forces and in Paris. The . . . [German] aim must, therefore, be to defeat the army in one or more major battles, capture Paris, and drive the remnants of the enemy's troops across the Loire. The most vulnerable area of France is that between Paris and Brussels, where the frontier is only 150 miles from the capital."[19] The French military leadership could not consider retreating into the interior of the country, conceding large portions of France to German occupation. French armies needed to fight along the frontiers, where Germany could inflict upon them battles of annihilation.

The major difficulty in attacking France was its extensive system of strong fortifications on the German frontier, which would greatly aid the defense. Behind this rampart the French army would frustrate any German plan for a "short and lively" war. Moreover, the lethality of modern rapid-fire weapons would devastate German assaults against the French defensive system. Schlieffen understood the benefits that the defender could accrue from firepower. His younger brother had died during the Franco-Prussian War during the murderous attack of the Prussian Guards Corps at the Battle of St. Privat.[20] Thus Schlieffen's plan entailed outflanking the French fortifications by making a gigantic flank march through Belgium and Holland. To ensure the success of the "right wing" in its march through the low countries, Schlieffen wanted to amass virtually the entire Germany army there. "It is essential [to the progress of the whole of the operations] to form a strong right wing," he wrote, "to win the battles with its help, to pursue the enemy relentlessly with this strong wing, forcing him to retreat again and again."[21] Under no circumstances, however, must the attack of the right wing come to a standstill. As long as the flank march through Belgium had sufficient forces, Schlieffen thought a quick victory over France was possible.

A second major consideration governing Schlieffen's strategic assessment was that Belgium offered a tempting path for attack. Belgium's army consisted of only six understrength, poorly equipped infantry divisions, and its fortresses were obsolete. These forces stood no chance of stopping a German power drive. Faced by a massive German invasion and the potential devastation that would stem from turning their country into a battle ground, the Belgian government might even consider not offering resistance and let Germany move its forces across their territory. After all, other countries faced with less daunting odds have tried to spare themselves the horrors of war by not fighting. It was not out of the question, then, that Belgium might jump on the German bandwagon when faced with the alternatives of fighting and losing or avoiding heavy losses by striking a deal with a strong neighbor. In addition to Belgian military weakness, Germany's rail network linked up with Belgium's system. Belgium's highly developed road and rail network made it possible for Germany to support logistically the movement of the armies that Schlieffen intended to deploy on the German right wing. Another factor made Belgium an attractive avenue for attacking France. French fortifications along the Belgian frontier were not as strong as those bordering on Germany. In these circumstances, German forces would stand a better chance of breaking French resistance.

A third strategic consideration for Schlieffen was Britain's apparent military weakness. Britain put an army of only seven front-line infantry divisions on the continent in 1914. By continental standards, this force appeared trivial to even the most astute strategic analysts. Bismarck is reputed to have quipped that, if the British army landed on Germany's North Sea coast, he would order out the police to arrest it. To Kaiser Wilhelm, Britain possessed a "contemptible" army. Moreover, British military performance during the Boer War did not impress foreign observers. Not understanding the difficulties inherent in fighting a determined force of irregulars, European military analysts downplayed the difficulties that faced Britain during the Boer War. While the British empire possessed considerable military potential, Britain could not mobilize it in time for the initial battles fought in France. Britain's navy, however, posed a serious threat to German trade. In a long war, British economic warfare could seriously hurt Germany's ability to wage war. Britain's Royal Navy, however, could not defend Paris, as Kaiser Wilhelm bluntly put it to French decision makers. Schlieffen and German military planners held a short time frame in their strategic calculations: they focused only a few months into the future. Since the full weight of Britain's strength would take longer to make itself felt, Germany's military leaders saw an opportunity to strike quickly to defeat France.

A final major strategic consideration was that Russia's army could not mount a powerful offensive into Germany during the early stages of a war. Russia's vast territorial expanse and sparse railway net inhibited a rapid concentration of Russian forces on the frontiers. Any German forces massed against Russia, unless they attacked onto Russian soil, would play a limited role during the opening stages of a two-front war. Germany possessed a window of opportunity to smash France before Russia could deploy and attack. Russia's lethargic operations during the Russo-Japanese War did not give the appearance of an aggressive adversary. The defeat in the Far East and the consequent revolutionary turmoil also meant that Russia posed next to no offensive threat to Germany when Schlieffen finalized his plan during the First Moroccan Crisis.

These vulnerabilities of Germany's enemies, Schlieffen argued, gave Germany a window of opportunity at the outbreak of a major war to attack France first, defeating it quickly, and then to turn against Russia. A preemptive attack held high risks but promised high rewards. If the German right wing could inflict heavy defeats on France's army during the initial period of operations, forcing a French withdrawal beyond the Loire, Germany's strategic position would improve considerably. With no possibility of France taking an offensive into Germany, Russia would also hesitate to attack. Germany and its ally Austria-Hungary would stand secure in the center of Europe: its adversaries possessing little chance to roll back German military gains. Faced with major German victories during the initial campaign, France and Russia might quickly come to terms.

On the Russian front, on the other hand, Schlieffen could not see a short war. If Germany struck against Russia first, the Russian armies might only retreat deep into the heart of the country. By avoiding major battles, the Russian army could protract the conflict. Mindful of Napoleon's catastrophic defeat in Russia in 1812, Schlieffen could not see a quick operational solution for defeating Russia. The very expanse of Russia's territory would frustrate any prospect for a short war and give France time to develop a powerful attack to invade Germany in the west. His inability to see any way of delivering a knockout blow against Russia reinforced Schlieffen's preference for making Germany's main effort against France in case of a two-front war.

On January 1, 1906, Helmuth von Moltke succeeded the 73–year-old Schlieffen as chief of the German general staff. A nephew of the victor of Königgrätz and Sedan, Moltke tried to refuse the post when Kaiser Wilhelm first offered it, saying: "Does your Majesty really think that you can twice win first prize in the same lottery?" Moltke insisted that, before accepting the position as chief of staff, the Kaiser must stop leading an army corps at maneuvers. The Kaiser's practice of assuming command of one side during maneuvers had made them into something of a joke, since he was expected to win. Moltke thought this precondition would result in the Kaiser appointing someone else. To Moltke's surprise, however, the Kaiser met his precondition.[22] This story sheds some light on Moltke's personality. In particular, it highlights a strange combination of stubbornness and tendency toward belittling himself; he also possessed an overly sensitive, moody, introspective character. The greatness of his uncle apparently haunted Moltke, since he often referred to himself as "the lesser thinker."[23] Despite his reputation among fellow officers as an "intellectual," Moltke did not really possess a powerful mind. Unlike other talented staff officers in Prussia's history—such as Schlieffen, the elder Moltke, Scharnhorst, and Clausewitz—he did not write tracts on military history or theory.

As chief of staff, Moltke accepted the strategic assumptions underlying Schlieffen's plan to attack France in the opening stages of the war. In at least two important respects, however, Moltke did modify the Schlieffen Plan. First, he decided against violating the neutrality of the Netherlands. Schlieffen thought that the rapid movement of the German right wing of armies required the violation of the neutrality of both Belgium and the Netherlands. Moltke disagreed. Instead, he concluded that the deployment of the German right wing could take place without the necessity of violating Dutch neutrality. This modification required that the Belgian fortress of Liege fall to a *coup de main*. Since Liege's fortifications lacked sufficient depth, Moltke thought that a surprise attack could overcome them. A special force of six brigades, supported by large-caliber howitzers, was kept in a state of constant readiness. This force, called the "Army of the Meuse," was to capture Liege immediately upon the outbreak of hostilities. Another consideration was that a neutral Holland could serve as a useful source of raw materials from the outside world if Britain began a blockade of Germany. Moltke called Holland the "windpipe" that would enable the German economy to breathe in the face of a British blockade.[24]

Secondly, Moltke decreased the strength of the German right wing that was to march through Belgium in relation to forces deployed in East Prussia and Lorraine. The resurgence of Russian military strength after the defeats of the Russo-Japanese War made it necessary for Moltke to modify the Schlieffen plan. An entire army, slated for the right wing marching through Belgium, went instead to defend East Prussia. Given the growth in Russia's military power, this reduction in the right wing's strength was probably unavoidable. In addition, Moltke reduced the German right wing even further to strengthen the left wing in Lorraine. He believed this necessary because of the increased combat power of the French army and the ascendancy of Grandmaison's *offensive à outrance* school of thought after 1911. Quite correctly, Moltke thought that the French army would advance out of its fortifications and launch an offensive in Lorraine. To meet this threat, Moltke concentrated two armies to fight what he thought would be a major and potentially decisive battle in Lorraine. Thus, the right wing, instead of having 37½ corps as envisioned by Schlieffen, possessed only 26 corps in 1914. Moltke had changed the fundamental shape of Germany's operational plan. Instead of a sweeping Napoleonic *manoeuvres sur les derrières*, the German plan called for a more even distribution of German forces across the entire breadth of front.[25]

Neither Conrad nor Moltke attempted at first to renew the contacts between the two staffs that had been broken off by Schlieffen. This changed, however, when the 1908 annexation of Bosnia-Herzegovina by Austria-Hungary provoked an international crisis.[26] Austria-Hungary's action raised the real prospect of war with Russia and Serbia. In December 1908, Conrad asked for permission to renew staff discussions with Germany, and on January 1, 1909, he began a high-level correspondence with Moltke.[27] The question foremost in Conrad's mind was what Germany's strategy would be in a war with France and Russia: would "Germany attack on both fronts simultaneously, or would it make its powerful main strike first against one and then the other adversary?" The answer to this question would help determine the strategy that the Habsburg Monarchy would employ in a war with Russia and Serbia.[28]

Conrad explained that, since the last contacts between the two general staffs, the strategic position of the Habsburg Monarchy had worsened. In particular, the growth in power of the Serbian state, with its irredentist claims against Austria-Hungary and its close ties with Russia, represented a major new military threat. In any future conflict with Russia, Conrad was certain that Austria-Hungary would also have to fight Serbia. On the other hand, if the Monarchy faced Serbia alone, the *"B"-Staffel* would go to the Balkans. With the *Minimalgruppe Balkan*, the forces of the *"B"-Staffel* would launch an offensive designed to destroy the Serbian army and overrun the

Balkan kingdom. The twenty-two infantry divisions *"B"-Staffel* and the *Minimalgruppe Balkan* would give Habsburg forces a two-to-one superiority over the Serbian army. Conrad did not intend to mobilize the *"A"-Staffel*. If Russia increased its military forces on the Monarchy's frontiers, however, the *"A"-Staffel* might deploy to Galicia as a precautionary measure. If Russia attacked, the *"B"-Staffel* would join the *"A"-Staffel* in Galicia. Meanwhile, the *Minimalgruppe Balkan* would stand on the defensive against Serbia. Once deployed in Galicia, the forty-two divisions of the *"A"-* and *"B"-Staffel* would attack into Russian Poland toward Lublin. Conrad pointed out a serious shortcoming in the Monarchy's military planning: if the partial mobilization against Serbia occurred, with the *"B"-Staffel* heading toward the Balkans, then this group could not be rapidly reversed and moved to Galicia in case of war with Russia. Russia might even decide to enter the war only after the deployment of the *"B"-Staffel* to the Balkans. Only the thirty divisions of the *"A"-Staffel*, then, would face the Russian army. If this scenario occurred, Conrad intended to stand on the defensive along the Carpathian mountain range and abandon most of Galicia. Only when the *"B"-Staffel* could return from the Balkans would Conrad consider taking the offensive against Russia. Conrad pointed out that the danger posed by Russia would decrease if the German army carried out an offensive in the east. Conrad confidently maintained that the *"A"-Staffel* alone could launch a successful offensive into Russian territory if Moltke promised to attack simultaneously with the German forces deployed in the east. The promise of a German offensive against Russia would even allow the retention of the *"B"-Staffel* in the Balkans to defeat Serbia. It is clear from this first letter between the two chiefs of staff that Conrad wanted to extract from Moltke a promise of an early German offensive against Russia. Furthermore, Conrad showed his desire for an early Habsburg offensive to overrun Serbia in a rapid campaign.[29]

Moltke's reply, dated January 21, contained little detailed information about the steps that Germany might take to help Austria-Hungary in the east in case of war. It was Moltke's opinion that the Entente powers would not risk war on Serbia's account. He assured Conrad that, if Russia attacked the Habsburg Monarchy, Germany would "stand with all its strength" behind its ally in full accord with the 1879 agreement. Furthermore, Germany would stand by Austria-Hungary in war with Russia even if it came about because of a Habsburg invasion of Serbia. Moltke, then, provided a different definition of the *casus foederis* than that used by Bismarck.

Without providing many details, Moltke rehearsed all the arguments against Germany making its main initial military effort against Russia. Since France's alliance commitments bound it to enter the war on Russia's side, Germany would face the threat of a French offensive in the west. It was Moltke's assessment that an equal division of German forces between the two fronts would be a "serious mistake." Instead, Moltke wanted to defend one front with a minimum of forces and amass as much military power as possible on the other. This concentration of forces on one front would enable him to carry out an offensive designed to achieve a quick decision. Since a defensive campaign in the west against France would require so many forces, Germany could not deploy in overwhelming numbers in the east. Moreover, Moltke argued that a rapid decision was not possible against Russia because of the vast theater of operations and unfavorable terrain. France, however, could be forced to fight a decisive battle: "There is no doubt that the French army will deploy along the border, if it does not itself attack. A decision must occur shortly after the deployment." Moltke refrained from telling Conrad that German forces would violate Belgium's neutrality, but he expressed confidence in a rapid victory over France. Once Germany had triumphed over France, Moltke promised the movements of strong forces to the east to support Austria-Hungary. Moltke also discounted Conrad's fear of Italy's entry into the war because the Italian army was so poorly equipped. Finally, Moltke thought that, before military operations in the east reached a turning point, the redeployment of German forces from France would occur. This redeployment would permit a full-scale German offensive against Russia. Since Germany intended to take attack after it redeployed its forces, Moltke urged Conrad to continue making preparations for a Habsburg offensive from Galicia.[30]

The message from Moltke confirmed Conrad's worst fears that only a small portion of the German army would initially deploy in the east to aid Austria-Hungary. Otherwise, Moltke supplied little information. In a follow-up letter, dated February 4, 1909, Conrad tried again to obtain more detailed information from Moltke. He specifically wanted to know what forces Germany intended to deploy in the east and whether they would take the offensive. Conrad put forward his assessment of the four possible courses that the initial stages of war might take. First, France might remain neutral while Russia attacked immediately. Second, France might stay neutral, with Russian military involvement occurring only after Austria-Hungary became engaged with Serbia. Third, France and Russia might attack at the outset of war. Finally, France and Russia might attack only after Austria-Hungary began fighting with Serbia. If the first two scenarios occurred, Conrad was not too concerned because he presumed that the bulk of German strength would deploy in the east. In the second scenario, the Habsburg armies would take the offensive against Russia even if only the "A"-Staffel was present in Galicia. If both France and Russia launched offensives immediately, both the "A"- and "B"-Staffel would deploy in Galicia. Meanwhile, Conrad expected the Germans to pin down the "19½ divisions of the Russian First (Niemen) and Second (Narew) Armies." It was the last scenario that particularly concerned Conrad. Under this scenario, Austria-Hungary would have only the "A"-Staffel deployed in Galicia. Conrad considered this scenario the "most dangerous" and the "most likely." Because of its likelihood, Conrad wanted to know when German reinforcements might arrive from the west. If he could not count on major German reinforcements by the fortieth day after Germany declared mobilization, Conrad intended to stay on the defensive in Galicia and meanwhile attack Serbia. Conrad wanted Moltke to answer three questions: What would Germany do if France remained neutral? What would she do in the east if both France and Russia entered the war? How soon after mobilization would German troops arrive in the east from the west?[31]

Conrad's letter cannot have pleased Moltke. The Schlieffen Plan, after all, was predicated on little Russian interference while Germany defeated France. In particular, Germany needed Austria-Hungary to tie down considerable Russian forces by an offensive from Galicia. Conrad's notions of striking down Serbia gained no support from Moltke: when Conrad first broached the subject in the January 1 letter Moltke wrote in the margin "secondary opponents should be treated as secondary."[32] In his reply dated February 24, Moltke agreed with Conrad's assessment that the scenario where both France and Russia initially refrained from action was the most difficult and yet most likely. In this situation, he promised the deployment of thirteen divisions in the east. Moltke asserted that "these German forces are strong enough to tie down on their own 19½ Russian divisions." With regard to when German reinforcements might arrive from the west, Moltke felt unable to answer with any certainty: "If France takes the offensive, the decision will come, in my opinion, within three weeks after mobilization. If the French army awaits our attack in the anticipated positions behind the frontier fortresses, then I expect a decision within four weeks." The transportation of reinforcements from France would require nine or ten more days. Moltke reminded Conrad, Germany and Austria-Hungary must first concentrate on defeating their primary opponents France and Russia. The destruction of Serbia, Moltke thought, must wait until after the defeat of their major adversaries. Next to this last comment Conrad wrote: "Certainly: but what am I to do if already tied down in Serbia?"[33]

In his next letter, dated March 8, 1909, Conrad decided he must force Moltke to give more concrete proposals concerning German military action. Specifically, he wanted a promise of a German offensive against Russia similar to the one given by the elder Moltke to Beck. Conrad planned to extract this pledge by withholding the prospect of a Habsburg offensive from Galicia. In a war with Russia and Serbia, Conrad promised to attack only if the *"B"- Staffel* managed to arrive in Galicia; if it went first to Serbia because of delayed Russian intervention, he would defend Galicia with the *"A"-Staffel* along the San and Dniester rivers. He would only attack with the thirty divisions of the *"A"-Staffel* if Moltke promised a German offensive across the Narew river into Russian Poland. To make clear the defensive

nature of this stance, Conrad sent along an accompanying map with the
positions of the *"A"-Staffel* sketched in along the San and Dniester.[34]

Conrad's letter placed Moltke in an awkward position. Moltke thought
that an offensive had no chance of success with only the thirteen divisions
left to face Russia under the Schlieffen Plan. On the other hand, if he refused
to pledge an early German offensive against Russia, he ran the risk of
alienating Conrad. Moltke wanted to avoid offending Conrad because he
considered it essential that a Habsburg offensive from Galicia draw Russian
forces away from Germany. In his reply of March 19, Moltke stressed that
the thirteen German divisions envisioned for deployment in East Prussia
would stand little chance of carrying out a successful offensive toward the
Narew. An attack would face the Russian army's superiority in numbers,
strong fortifications, and unfavorable terrain. Germany's forces would have
a difficult enough time defending East Prussia from a Russian attack. A
German offensive toward the Narew under these circumstances would
likely end in disaster. "Nevertheless," Moltke replied, "I will not hesitate to
undertake an attack in order to support a simultaneous Austrian offensive.
Your Excellency can count absolutely upon this pledge." He added the
reservation, however, that enemy action might make it impossible to carry
out the offensive. Moltke, then, had left himself an escape route to get out
of his pledge.[35]

Conrad, however, thought that this pledge had bound the Germans to
an early offensive in the east. Because of Moltke's promise, it no longer
appeared to matter to Conrad whether the *"B"- Staffel* initially went to the
Serbian front. If the *"B"-Staffel* went to the Balkans, it might as well remain
there and smash Serbia in a rapid campaign. Thus, by 1909, Conrad intended to begin the next war by launching simultaneous offensives on both
the Serbian and Russian fronts. He doesn't seem to have regarded this
division of strength as dangerous; nor does he seem to have taken seriously
the reservation added by Moltke to his pledge. On April 10, 1909, Conrad
closed this part of his prewar correspondence with Moltke, saying that he
held the pledges given in this correspondence as binding, and he intended
to use them as the basis for future planning.[36]

The 1909 correspondence forms the most important part of the prewar
military collaboration between the two chiefs of staff. Although Moltke and
Conrad continued their correspondence until the outbreak of the war, the
commitments they made during the Bosnian Crisis remained the corner-
stone of prewar cooperation. Both Moltke and Conrad felt satisfied with the
results of this initial collaboration. Conrad had received assurances that
ended his fears about a two-front war with Serbia and Russia. Moltke, too,
had benefited: he could now depend on an offensive by Austria-Hungary
that should distract Russian forces from Germany.

Yet these discussions also promoted the possibility of great miscalculation in a conflict with the Entente powers. Agreement between the two

chiefs of staff had only come about because of Moltke's reservation. More-over, the German chief of staff saw it as an escape clause that permitted him to renege on his commitment to launch an early offensive. Moltke must surely have surmised that he would probably have to invoke this reserva-tion in case of a showdown with Russia: why else would he have stressed the difficulties of an offensive into Russian Poland? Conrad, on the other hand, minimized the importance of the reservation made by Moltke. He continued to labor on plans for his army to attack on two fronts simultane-ously since he trusted in a German offensive to divert the Russians. In making these pledges, both sides were exploiting their ally to the fullest to gain their own individual objectives. Conrad meant to strike down the Serbian threat to the Monarchy at the outbreak of the next war, just as Radetzky had humbled Italian pretensions in 1848 and 1849. Meanwhile, Moltke would go ahead with the Schlieffen Plan without worrying too much about his rear. Only one question remained: who would be left to fight Russia?

Moltke recognized that achieving agreement on a common strategy for Austria-Hungary and Germany had only occurred because he and Conrad papered over their differences. Consequently, Moltke tried to persuade the Habsburg general staff of the strategic wisdom of concentrating all their available forces in Galicia and undertaking an early offensive. In a letter written on February 10, 1912, Moltke urged Conrad to throw all his forces in case of a general European war against Russia. Meanwhile, Germany intended to concentrate on the rapid defeat of France. In Moltke's opinion, Germany's campaign against France would decide the outcome of a general European war. Thus, Moltke concluded that "the destiny of Austria will be decided not on the Bug, but on the Seine."[37]

Moltke's view that Germany should concentrate the overwhelming bulk of its army against France had received confirmation from a war game conducted by the German general staff in 1912. In this staff exercise, German planners reverted to the ideas of the elder Moltke and concentrated approxi-mately half their forces, or eighteen army corps, against Russia. These forces, together with Habsburg armies attacking out of Galicia, launched powerful offensives that overran Congress Poland within thirty-five days of the proclamation of mobilization. These successes did not result in a rapid end to the war. Although German and Habsburg armies gained considerable territory, they did not succeed in destroying Russia's armies. Instead, the Russian armies avoided a decisive defeat and retreated to a line running from Vilna to Kiev. Moreover, while Russian armies kept half the German army tied down in the east, French armies attacking in Lorraine had gained the upper hand in the west. By the forty-fifth day after mobili-zation, the German fortified positions around Metz were in danger of being outflanked by French forces. This exercise only highlighted the danger for

Germany of initially attacking Russia and leaving the strategic initiative in the west to the French.[38]

Not surprisingly, Conrad saw the strategic situation differently from German war planners: he would not be deterred from his notion of crushing the Serbian menace; in his view, Austria-Hungary's fate depended on the outcome of battles fought along the Sava and Danube. Thus, Conrad and Moltke never reconciled their divergent strategic views. This goes a long way toward explaining the defeats suffered by Austria-Hungary and Germany in the opening campaigns of the war.

To be sure, their common fear of Russia's growing military prowess caused both Conrad and Moltke to favor a preventive war to break the strategic encirclement of the Central Powers. Conrad persisted in urging that the Monarchy attack Serbia. He did not believe that the Monarchy's diplomatic and strategic situation would improve in the future—he thought it might get much worse. Consequently, Conrad forcefully urged a war against Serbia in the wake of the Second Balkan War. Before Serbia could consolidate its recently acquired territorial gains, Conrad thought the Monarchy must strike. He thought that the rapid recovery by the Russian army made it unlikely that Russia would stand aside and allow a localized war between Austria-Hungary and Serbia. Conrad told Count Kageneck, the German military attaché, in January 1914, that Russia would surely attack Austria-Hungary in case it went to war with Serbia. He added: "One might almost wish for it [Russia] to attack soon because our position is unlikely to improve." Of course, Conrad preferred that any conflict with Serbia remain confined to the Balkans. Moltke agreed with Conrad's pessimistic assessment. When the two chiefs of staff met at Karlsbad in May 1914, Moltke wanted to begin a great war before their enemies grew too strong.[39] In particular, Russia's increasing ability for rapid deployment called into question the viability of the Schlieffen Plan.[40]

Yet, while both chiefs of staff wanted to wage a preventive war, it is significant that they disagreed about the form this conflict should take. Conrad's stare remained fixed on the Balkans; Moltke, meanwhile, aimed at defeating France in a single campaign. These divergent views on the objectives of a preventive war illustrate the political differences between Austria-Hungary and Germany. Moreover, the inability to agree on basic strategic goals runs counter to the conclusions reached by some historians of the Fischer school, who argue that Conrad and Moltke possessed a precise blueprint for aggression.[41] The prewar correspondence between Conrad and Moltke does not reveal any long-term plot—that is, a precise agenda—for an aggressive war against the Entente powers. Instead, it shows a strategic incoherence and lack of agreement on plans by the two military chiefs.[42]

Far from changing the nature of the alliance between Austria-Hungary and Germany, the staff talks between Conrad and Moltke reinforced their complacency about the efficacy of existing war plans. Perhaps the greatest danger of these talks was that they confirmed the underlying strategic assumptions of Conrad and Moltke. This meant that Conrad's strategic gaze would initially focus on the Balkans, while Moltke looked to deliver a knockout blow against France by employing the Schlieffen Plan. The staff talks had the paradoxical effect of reducing real military collaboration between Austria-Hungary and Germany. Both Conrad and Moltke lulled themselves into thinking that they need not change their war plans. Each wanted to entrap the other. This thinking was dangerous, given the military improvements made by Britain, France, Russia, and Serbia, and the increased cooperation between them. The opening campaigns of the First World War show that Austria-Hungary and Germany did a poor job of coordinating their military plans. Consequently, the Central Powers failed to achieve the best strategic results with the resources available. For Austria-Hungary, the squandering of its military power in divergent offensives was to produce catastrophic consequences for its internal cohesion and standing as an independent great power.

NOTES

1. Ludwig Beck, "West- oder Ost-Offensive 1914?" in *Studien*, ed. Hans Speidel (Stuttgart: K. F. Koehler Verlag, 1955), 158.

2. For the preparations of the Entente, see Samuel R. Williamson, *The Politics of Grand Strategy: Britain and France Prepare for War, 1904–1914* (Cambridge: Harvard University Press, 1969).

3. On Austrian foreign policy in this era, see Alfred F. Pribram, *Austrian Foreign Policy, 1908–1918* (London: George Allen and Unwin, 1923); O. H. Wedel, *Austro-German Diplomatic Relations, 1908–1914* (Stanford: Stanford University Press, 1932); and Solomon Wank, "Aehrenthal and the Policy of Action" (Ph.D. diss., Columbia University, 1961).

4. Gordon A. Craig, *The Politics of the Prussian Army, 1640–1945* (Oxford: Oxford University Press, 1955), 289.

5. For a thorough account of the detailed military and naval staff talks between Britain and France, see Williamson, *Politics of Grand Strategy*, 59–88, 167–204, 227–48, 264–83, 300–27. The degree of coordination achieved by the British army and navy staffs with their French counterparts in war plans would have surprised the majority of the British cabinet. There is no detailed, scholarly account examining the military and naval cooperation between France and Russia for the period between 1906 and 1914. Perhaps the best account in English is by L.C.F. Turner, "The Russian Mobilization in 1914," in *The War Plans of the Great Powers, 1880–1914*, ed. Paul Kennedy (London: George Allen and Unwin, 1979), 252–60. But this account must be supplemented by D.C.B. Lieven, *Russia and the Origins of the First World War* (New York: St. Martin's Press, 1983), 102–19.

6. The classic exposition of Bismarck's diplomacy during this period is William L. Langer, *European Alliances and Alignments, 1871–1890*, 2d ed. (New York: Alfred A. Knopf, 1966); a more recent examination of Austro-German relations is

provided by Nicholas der Bagdasarian, *The Austro-German Rapprochement, 1870–1879: From the Battle of Sedan to the Dual Alliance* (Rutherford, N.J.: Fairleigh Dickinson University Press, 1976).

7. On these initial meetings between the two staffs, see Gerhard Ritter, *The Schlieffen Plan: Critique of a Myth*, trans. Andrew and Eva Wilson (New York: Praeger, 1958), 18–22; Craig, *Politics of the Prussian Army*, 273–77; Gerhard Ritter, "Die Zusammenarbeit der Generalstäbe Deutschlands und Oesterreich-Ungarns vor dem ersten Weltkrieg," in *Zur Geschichte und Problematik der Demokratie: Festgabe für Hans Herzfeld* (Berlin: Duncker und Humblot, 1958), 523–49; Ronald Louis Ernharth, "The Tragic Alliance: Austro-German Military Cooperation, 1871–1918" (Ph.D. diss., Columbia University, 1970), 15–56; and, for the Habsburg perspective, see von Glaise-Horstenau, *Franz Josephs Weggefährte*.

8. In addition to strategic considerations, Moltke was essentially pro-Austrian in his political orientation during this period, see Eberhard Kessel, *Moltke* (Stuttgart: K. F. Koehler Verlag, 1957), 708–9.

9. Graf von Moltke, *Die deutschen Aufmarschpläne, 1871–1890, Forschungen und Darstellungen aus dem Reichsarchiv*, volume vii, ed. D. von Schmerfeld (Berlin: E. S. Mittler und Sohn, 1929), 77.

10. Langer, *European Alliances and Alignments*, 412–13.

11. Ritter, *Schlieffen Plan*, 28.

12. Ibid., 23.

13. For a lucid examination of Napoleon's operational use of the *manoeuvres sur les derrières*, see David Chandler, *The Campaigns of Napoleon* (New York: Macmillan, 1966), 161–78, 264–86, 382–402.

14. See Lothar Höbelt, "Schlieffen, Beck, Potiorek und das Ende der gemeinsamen deutsch-österreichisch-ungarischen Aufmarschpläne im Osten," *Militärgeschichtliche Mitteilungen*, 2 (1984): 7–30.

15. Ritter, *Schlieffen Plan*, 31; Glaise-Horstenau, *Franz Josephs Weggefährte*, 346–56.

16. R. R. Palmer, "Frederick the Great, Guibert, Bülow: From Dynastic to National War," *Makers of Modern Strategy*, ed. Edward Mead Earle (Princeton: Princeton University Press, 1943), 58.

17. On German strategy in this era, see the provocative essays by Holger H. Herwig, "From the Tirpitz Plan to Schlieffen Plan: Some Observations on German Military Planning," *The Journal of Strategic Studies*, 9, 1 (1986): 53–63; Dennis E. Showalter, "The Eastern Front and German Military Planning, 1871–1914: Some Observations," *East European Quarterly*, 15, 2 (1981): 163–80; and idem, "German Grand Strategy: A Contradiction in Terms?" *Militärgeschichtliche Mitteilungen* (1990): 75–82; and Gunther E. Rothenberg, "Moltke, Schlieffen, and the Doctrine of Strategic Envelopment," in *Makers of Modern Strategy*, ed. Peter Paret (Princeton: Princeton University Press, 1986), 324 ff.

18. Ritter, *Schlieffen Plan*, 172.

19. Clausewitz, *On War*, 633–34.

20. Bucholz, *Moltke, Schlieffen*, 120.

21. Ibid., 144.

22. Helmuth von Moltke, *Erinnerungen, Briefe, Dokumente, 1877–1916* (Stuttgart: Der Kommende Tag A. G., 1922), 308–10.

23. For a perceptive picture of Moltke's personality, see Correlli Barnett, *The Swordbearers: Supreme Command in the First World War* (Bloomington, Ind.: Indiana University Press, 1963), 3–98.

24. Ritter, *Schlieffen Plan*, 106. In addition, see the excellent study of German prewar economic preparations done by Avner Offer, *The First World War: An Agrarian Interpretation* (Oxford: Clarendon Press, 1991), 319–53.

25. Ibid., 138–39.

26. The best treatment of the Bosnian crisis remains Bernadotte E. Schmitt, *The Annexation of Bosnia, 1908–1909* (Cambridge: Cambridge University Press, 1937).

27. *AMD*, i, 367–70, provides details about the opening of these discussions between Conrad and Moltke. Aehrenthal and the German chancellor Prince Bernard Bülow arranged them beforehand. Throughout the correspondence between the two chiefs of staff, the Habsburg foreign minister, the German chancellor, and the two emperors saw the letters. Before beginning this correspondence, Conrad and Moltke had met earlier in May 1907 on a visit by Archduke Franz Ferdinand to Berlin where he viewed German army maneuvers. Nothing more came of this formal meeting, however, except a vague acknowledgment between the two that closer cooperation was necessary. See *AMD*, i, 69. With very few exceptions, the Conrad-Moltke correspondence is reproduced in Conrad's memoirs. On this prewar correspondence, see the brilliant articles by Norman Stone, "Moltke-Conrad: Relations Between the Austro-Hungarian and German General Staffs, 1909–1914," *The Historical Journal*, 9, 2 (1966); and Holger H. Herwig, "Disjointed Allies: Coalition Warfare in Berlin and Vienna, 1914," *The Journal of Military History*, 54 (1990): 265–80. In addition, see the detailed studies by Graydon A. Tunstall, *Planning for War Against Russia and Serbia: Austro-Hungarian and German Military Strategies, 1871–1914* (Boulder, Colo.: Social Science Monographs, 1993); and Ronald Louis Ernharth, "The Tragic Alliance: Austro-German Military Cooperation, 1871–1918" (Ph.D. diss., Columbia University, 1970).

28. *AMD*, i, 632.

29. Ibid., 633–34. Conrad also voiced his fear that Italy would seize the opportunity of a general European war to attack the Habsburg Monarchy. Once again, Conrad displayed his concern about the great danger that the Habsburg Monarchy faced in the irredentist claims of Italy and Serbia.

30. Ibid., *380–84*.

31. Ibid., 385–92.

32. *Weltkrieg*, ii, 8.

33. *AMD*, i, 394–96.

34. Ibid., 396–99. See Stone, "Moltke-Conrad," 214.

35. *AMD*, i, 403–5.

36. Ibid., 405.

37. *AMD*, iii, 145.

38. See Jack Snyder, *The Ideology of the Offensive: Military Decision Making and the Disasters of 1914* (Ithaca, N.Y.: Cornell University Press, 1984), 117; and conversation with Dennis Showalter, December 13, 1988.

39. *AMD*, iii, 596.

40. D. N. Collins, "The Franco-Russian Alliance and Russian Railways, 1891–1914," *The Historical Journal*, 16 (1973): 777–88. On public attitudes in Austria-Hungary and Germany about the growth of Russian power, see Risto Ropponen, *Die*

russische Gefahr: Das Verhalten der öffentlichen Meinung Deutschlands und Österreich-Ungarns gegenüber der Aussenpolitik Russlands in der Zeit zwischen dem Frieden von Portsmouth und dem Ausbruch des Erstens Weltkriegs (Helsinki: Suomen Histori-allinen Seura, 1976).

41. For this view of Conrad's and Moltke's actions, see the two articles by Adolf Gasser, "Der deutsche Hegemonialkrieg von 1914," in *Deutschland in der Weltpolitik des 19. und 20. Jahrhunderts: Festschrift für Fritz Fischer*, ed. Imanuel Geiss and Bernd Jürgen Wendt (Düsseldorf: Bertelsmann Universitätsverlag, 1973), 310 ff.; and "Deutschlands Entschluss zum Präventivkrieg 1913–1914," in *Discordia Concors: Festschrift für Edgar Bonjour*, ed. Marc Sieber (Basel: Helbing and Lichten-hahn, 1968), 173 ff.

42. It is somewhat ironic, but the navies of Germany and Austria-Hungary proved more successful in putting together a common strategy for wartime than did the armies. On the negotiations between Germany, Austria-Hungary, and Italy for naval cooperation, see Paul G. Halpern, *The Mediterranean Naval Situation, 1908–1914* (Cambridge: Harvard University Press, 1971), 220–79.

Part Two

The July Crisis

Chapter 4

A Terrorist Attack in Sarajevo: Austria-Hungary and Germany Decide for War

THE OUTRAGE IN SARAJEVO

The June 28, 1914 assassination of Franz Ferdinand and his wife in Sarajevo by the Bosnian terrorist Gavrilo Princip triggered the chain reaction known as the July Crisis that culminated in the outbreak of general war between the European great powers. Despite the vast literature on the outbreak of the First World War, perhaps no aspect of this tragedy remains clouded in as much mystery, speculation, and political bias as the actual plot to murder the heir apparent to the throne of the Habsburg Monarchy.[1] Sir Edward Grey, Britain's foreign secretary, called Princip's offense the perfect political murder since the truth surrounding its origins and its implementation would probably never be known.[2]

With the passage of time, however, more details of the assassination plot have surfaced, and it is now possible to reconstruct the degree of the Serbian government's involvement in the murder of Franz Ferdinand. The assassination was the work of extreme Serbian nationalists living in Serbia and Bosnia. Bosnian Serb extremists wanted to bring about the union of Bosnia with a greater Serbia. Serbia's military intelligence helped in organizing a terrorist campaign targeted against officials of the Habsburg Monarchy. Dragutin Dimitrijević, who used the code name Apis, the head of Serbian military intelligence, masterminded this terrorist campaign. He ensured the provision of arms, explosives, training, and safe passage across Austria-Hungary's border with Serbia. With his assistance, a terrorist network was established. The goal of this terrorist campaign was to provoke increasing clashes within the Habsburg Monarchy between southern Slav ethnic groups and the government. By attempting to sharpen the alienation felt by the Slavic peoples of the Monarchy, Apis aimed at undermining Habsburg rule. His goal was to destroy any chance for internal political reform within Austria-Hungary and pave the way for an enlarged Serbian kingdom.

Mounting unrest, caused by an escalating cycle of terrorist violence and counter-terrorist repression, would radicalize the southern Slav peoples within the Habsburg Monarchy. Beset and weakened by large-scale civil unrest, the Monarchy might prove ripe for a war of partition. Other states with irredentist claims—such Romania, Italy, perhaps even Russia—would jump on the bandwagon, joining Serbia in the conflict and benefiting from the collapse of Habsburg power.[3] The success of the Balkan states in driving the vestigial remains of Turkish rule out of Europe augured for the success of this program to dismember Austria-Hungary.

The Serbian government of Prime Minister Nikola Pašić did not approve of this terrorist campaign nor any assassination plot to kill Franz Ferdinand. Pašić, however, could not press his opposition too far without putting his own government in danger. The same terrorist organizations that wanted to topple Habsburg rule in Bosnia could also strike against the Belgrade government. To prevent Pašić from foiling his plans, Dimitrijević even went so far as to plot a coup to overthrow the Serbian government. Although Dimitrijević's terrorist program increased the risk of involving Serbia in a war with Austria-Hungary, Pašić was intimidated by the prospect of a coup. His government could do little to stop the planned strike against Franz Ferdinand. The Serbian government thus turned a blind eye and tacitly support the terrorists. When the Serbian government garnered information about the plot to assassinate Franz Ferdinand, it did try to alert Vienna of the danger. But Belgrade's warning went unheeded because it was made in an opaque way to avoid the embarrassment of having to admit to the role played by the Serbian military intelligence service. It is little wonder, then, that Habsburg officials did not pay much attention.

That the terrorists succeeded, however, was due in large part to the grotesque incompetence of Habsburg officials in Sarajevo. In particular, the blunders of the governor general of Bosnia-Herzegovina, General Oskar Potiorek, gave the assassins their opportunity to kill Franz Ferdinand. The visit of Franz Ferdinand to Sarajevo had been publicly known for over three months. The knowledge of the impending visit provided time to assemble a group of seven terrorists in the city. One failed bomb attempt showed plainly the danger to the heir apparent. Yet, Potiorek did little to provide for extra security. To supplement the approximately 150 policemen on guard, Potiorek could have called in some of the 70,000 soldiers on maneuvers outside of Sarajevo. But this security measure was rejected because the soldiers' uniforms were muddy, and they might create a poor impression for the populace. Concern for spit and polish, then, stood in the way of providing for Franz Ferdinand's security. Instead, it was decided to take the sensible precaution of changing the route of the official motorcade. The only problem was that no one bothered to tell the drivers of the cars in the motorcade of the change! When the driver of Franz Ferdinand's car did not follow the new route, Potiorek ordered him to stop in an attempt to clear up the confusion in plans. This confusion gave Princip his opportunity to strike. With the official party stopped right in front of him, Princip walked onto the street from the sidewalk, brushing past a police officer, and stepped onto the running board of Franz Ferdinand's car. Princip fired point blank at the heir apparent and his wife, fatally wounding both of them. A modicum of better security preparations could have prevented the assassination. The outbreak of war in 1914 hinged on an improbable series of blunders on the part of Habsburg officials.

VIENNA'S REACTION

Whatever the actual circumstances that led to the Sarajevo outrage, the reaction of decision makers in Vienna and Berlin was that the murder of Franz Ferdinand formed part of a widespread conspiracy involving the Serbian government. Furthermore, this provocation of state-sponsored terrorism justified military action against Serbia. The German ambassador, Count Heinrich von Tschirschky, reported to Berlin the animosity against Serbia that he found in Vienna: "I frequently hear expressed here, even among serious people, the wish [that] at *last a final and fundamental reckoning should be had with the Serbs.*"[4]

During the preceding Balkan crisis, these voices calling for war had been held in check by the heir apparent Franz Ferdinand. Now his assassination changed dramatically the political balance within Austria-Hungary. During the preceding diplomatic crises, Franz Ferdinand had stood against provoking war with Serbia and Russia. In Habsburg decision making, his voice was paramount in keeping in line those that wanted to force a showdown. Franz Ferdinand's political program was that of reform within the Monarchy, particularly that of curbing the power of the Hungarian magnates. To accomplish his program, he was ready to use force within the Monarchy; he even contemplated and was prepared for the outbreak of a civil war with Hungary. Franz Ferdinand, however, did not aim to solve the Monarchy's domestic problems by starting a war with foreign powers. It is simply wrong, then, to consider Franz Ferdinand "the leader of Austria's war party," or "a strong supporter of a preventive war against Serbia."[5] Whatever his faults as a leader, the heir apparent did not consider a war with Serbia and Russia worth the risks or offering a solution to the Habsburg Monarchy's internal political problems. The death of Franz Ferdinand eliminated an important voice calling for prudence in foreign policy. Furthermore, his assassination strengthened the hands of those within the Habsburg Monarchy who wanted to provoke a conflict with Serbia.

Foremost among those who wanted war was the chief of the general staff, Conrad von Hötzendorf. He first heard the news of the assassination late in the day on June 28. In Conrad's opinion, the assassination "was not the act of isolated fanatics, it was the work of a well-organized attack, it was the declaration of war by Serbia on Austria-Hungary."[6] Writing to his future wife on the day of the assassination, Conrad confessed his fears about provoking war. Nonetheless, he saw no alternative for dealing with the conspiracy that he saw encircling the Monarchy.

The assassination has a pronounced Serbian nationalist character and is an out-growth of the political agitation that has already subverted our South Slav territo-ries. Therein lies—completely ignored by the pure humanitarians—the dark political importance of this outrage. . . .

What consequences the assassination will have cannot yet be envisioned—whether it remains an isolated act or whether it is part of a well-prepared larger action, we cannot decide for the present.

Unfortunately I have formed the opinion that nothing good can be envisioned for the future of the Monarchy, especially for the near future. Serbia and Romania will be nails in her coffin—Russia will vigorously promote them at the same time; it will be a hopeless struggle, but it must be waged because such an old Monarchy and such a glorious army cannot go under in shame.[7]

When Conrad returned to Vienna from Karlstadt on June 29, he pressed for a military response to the assassination in Sarajevo. Despite his forebod-ing about the Monarchy's strategic predicament, he wanted to go to war with Serbia immediately. He told his staff, who waited for him in the war ministry offices, "that the assassination was a Serbian machination, which had created an extremely serious situation and would lead to war with Serbia; thereby bringing forward the danger that Russia and Romania would have to be counted as enemies."[8]

Later the same day Conrad met with foreign minister Count Berchtold to urge the necessity of prompt military action.[9] Conrad later recounted in his memoirs that Berchtold agreed about the utility of military action. Before starting a war with Serbia, however, Berchtold wanted three precon-ditions met.[10] First, Berchtold wanted a guarantee of Germany's diplomatic support because a quarrel with Serbia carried with it the potential for a confrontation with Russia. Since Kaiser Wilhelm was expected to attend the upcoming state funeral of Franz Ferdinand, Berchtold intended to use this opportunity for high-level discussions with German decision makers. As it turned out, Wilhelm did not attend Franz Ferdinand's funeral.[11] Conse-quently, Vienna dispatched to Berlin Count Alexander Hoyos of the foreign ministry to canvass the views of German decision makers and obtain Germany's support for a showdown with Serbia. But Berchtold made clear to Conrad that, only if he could be certain of Germany's support would he enter war with Serbia. Second, Berchtold was concerned that in the public opinion the Monarchy was not prepared for war. In particular, Berchtold feared that mobilization might trigger a revolt among the Czechs. Thus, Berchtold wanted to make certain that the Monarchy built public support for war. Berchtold's final precondition was that he wanted to orchestrate the confrontation with Serbia in a step-by-step manner, in which military would be the last step. Under Berchtold's game plan, an attack against Serbia would occur only after a formal investigation of the assassination and the presentation of an ultimatum to Belgrade. This ultimatum would include a formal list of demands, such as the dissolution of anti-Habsburg societies and the firing of the Serbian Minister of Police. Berchtold expected Belgrade to reject these demands. Once that occurred, Austria-Hungary would militarily move against Serbia.

Conrad disagreed almost completely with Berchtold's assessment of the situation. To be sure, Conrad thought that Germany's support was desirable. But he argued that Austria-Hungary should not wait for Berlin's consent before ordering mobilization. Conrad insisted on ordering mobilization at once because the "assassination had been a blow against the Monarchy that ought to be followed by immediate measures." In any event, Conrad thought war inevitable, so mobilization should take place as soon as possible. Conrad also argued that the assassination of a member of the Monarchy's royal family would hardly endear Serbia to the ruling heads in Russia and Romania. Thus, because the assassination was directed against the monarchic principle, Serbia would be diplomatically isolated. With regard to Berchtold's second precondition, Conrad thought public opinion was already in favor of war. He sought to calm Berchtold's fears that a revolution might occur in Bohemia. Moreover, Conrad pointed out that the Croats and Moslems within the Monarchy were hostile to the Serbs. Finally, Conrad did not believe that Berchtold's list of demands would amount to any concrete improvement in Serbia's behavior toward the Monarchy. Conrad told Berchtold: "The Serbs will quietly dismiss the Minister of Police; it will have no effect at all; nothing will have effect but the use of force." Only a victorious war, in Conrad's estimation, would solve the problem posed by Serbia.

According to Berchtold's account of the conversation, Conrad blamed the current crisis on the failed policies of the previous foreign minister, Alois von Aehrenthal. Conrad said that Aehrenthal should have moved against Serbia during previous confrontations with Belgrade, when the Monarchy's strategic position was relatively stronger. To avoid a repeat of past foreign policy failures, Conrad asked for permission to mobilize immediately against Serbia. Strong military measures were required, in Conrad's view, because with Serbia one "had a poisonous viper at your feet, thus one steps on its head and does not wait for the deadly bite." Berchtold recalled that "with an air of sadness, on that elegant, pallid countenance, he [Conrad] ended momentously with the three words: 'War, War, War!' "[12] What these and subsequent discussions illustrate is the strong streak of fatalism running through Conrad's policy recommendations. Throughout the July Crisis, Conrad pushed for war, although he thought the chances of the Monarchy in war were not good. Samuel Williamson speculates that Conrad's constant refrain of an immediate war with Serbia might be due in part to the general's obsessive love for Gina von Reininghaus, a woman twenty-eight years his junior. By obtaining military glory, Conrad thought he might overcome Habsburg society's disapproval of a marriage to her. According to Williamson, "a hero's welcome [for Conrad] following a military victory might offer the possibility of marrying Gina." In pushing for and obtaining a showdown with Serbia, "Conrad had got his war and his wife." Yet Conrad was not alone in pressing for war during the summer of 1914. The entire senior military leadership wanted to provoke a conflict with Serbia, and the foreign ministry thought it was an opportune moment to enhance Austria-Hungary's security in the Balkans. Thus, there was more to Conrad's motivations for war than his libido. That Serbian military intelligence was believed to have instigated the assassination of Franz Ferdinand is explanation enough for Conrad's bellicosity.[13] Conrad recognized that Austria-Hungary faced long odds in provoking a war with Serbia. He told an old friend: "In the years 1908–9, it would have been a game where we held all the strong cards; in 1912–13, a game with the odds in our favor; now it is nothing more than a gamble."[14] Serbia's state-sponsored terrorist attack, in Conrad's view, demanded a military response by Austria-Hungary.

The next morning, the war minister, Alexander von Krobatin, met with Berchtold after arriving back in Vienna from a military inspection in the Tyrol. Berchtold later recalled that Krobatin "was fire and flames for war as the last and only way out. The army was ready."[15] Conrad reinforced Krobatin's message on July 1, when the chief of staff again pressed his views on Berchtold. According to Conrad, Berchtold wanted to delay military action against Serbia until after the investigation of the assassination was completed and evidence turned up of Belgrade's complicity. Furthermore, Berchtold feared that a war against Serbia would lead to Russia's intervention. If that occurred, both Germany and Romania might defect from the side of Austria-Hungary. Berchtold considered it a real possibility that Austria-Hungary might face Russia alone in this crisis. At all cost, he wanted to avoid putting the Monarchy in a position of diplomatic isolation. In reply, Conrad "took the point of view that only a display of force could avert that threat from Serbia. The murder committed under Serbian patronage was the grounds for war." As to Berchtold's fears about diplomatic isolation, Conrad conceded that "Germany and Romania might leave us in the lurch." If that did occur, then Austria-Hungary's "hands were certainly tied." Even Conrad, then, did not consider it strategically feasible for Austria-Hungary to fight single-handed against both Serbia and Russia. He reassured Berchtold, however, that Germany would "cover our rear against Russia."[16] Thus, the two highest military authorities of the Monarchy counseled Berchtold that, since war with Serbia was inevitable, mobilization and military action should occur immediately.

Later on July 1, Berchtold requested that Conrad prepare a short memorandum, laying out what military consequences "the neutrality and possible hostility of Romania would have in a European war" for the Monarchy and its Triple Alliance partners, Germany and Italy. Conrad promptly replied the following day in a memorandum for Franz Joseph and Kaiser Wilhelm.[17] The Romanian army figured prominently in Conrad's net assessment of the military balance existing between the Monarchy and Russia in Galicia. If the Romanian army concentrated against Russia in Bessarabia, it could tie down three Russian army corps. With these Russian forces tied down on the Romanian frontier—the equivalent of an entire army—Russia's numerical superiority over Habsburg forces would dwindle to the point where Russia was unlikely to carry out a successful offensive into Galicia.

On the other hand, if Romania remained neutral, Russia would possess another army for operations against Galicia. This contingency would undercut Conrad's plans to conduct an offensive against Serbia in the Balkans. Conrad pessimistically said that "the more favorable case of simple neutrality by Romania would be equivalent to the loss of 20 divisions, that is, about 400,000 men, while the entry of Romania into the ranks of the enemies of the Triple Alliance would mean a loss to us of 40 divisions, that is about 800,000 men." This last possibility gravely affected the Monarchy's military position against Russia. "Until now in a Triple Alliance war," Conrad wrote, "the Austro-Hungarian army has had to bear the main burden of the fight against Russia, to make it possible for the allied German army to win quickly a decisive victory over France. This difficult task for our main forces had prospect of success only so long as the cooperation of the Romanian army could be counted on." In effect, Romania's army held the balance between Habsburg and Russian forces in Galicia: if Romania remained neutral, Russia could mass the forces to carry out an offensive into Galicia, while Habsburg plans for an attack into Russian Poland would be compromised by superior Russian forces.

An even more dangerous situation would occur if Romania joined with Russia and Serbia in an attack on the Monarchy. The military intervention of Romania on the side of Russia and Serbia would heighten the nationalist aspirations of Romanians living within the Monarchy. In addition, a Romanian attack might result in the military occupation of Transylvania. More important, Romania's intervention would "decisively influence the main fighting forces of Austria-Hungary in the primary theater of war against Russia if the Romanian army, possibly in cooperation with Serbian military forces, presses forward without halting . . . into the center of the Monarchy." Conrad recommended that defensive precautions be immediately undertaken in Transylvania in case of Romanian hostility: "Since the Monarchy must in the future be more than ever determined to concentrate all forces on the decisive main blow against Russia, it is urgently necessary to block all road and rail communications leading from Romania into the Monarchy by permanent fortifications to prevent an unhindered invasion of Transylvania." Only an open treaty of alliance between Romania and the Monarchy "could count as a guarantee against possible hostility" and make these defensive measures unnecessary. "The slightest doubt on this point would make it imperative to take military precautions without delay."

Conrad attached to this memorandum a table showing the clear military inferiority of Austria-Hungary and its allies in a general European war. In this table, Conrad listed Romania's twenty divisions in the camp of the Entente. The military balance would further tilt in the favor of the Entente if Italy's thirty-four divisions were not included on the side of the Triple Alliance. In the text of the memorandum, Conrad drew special attention to Italy's military weakness: "The numerical comparison of the combined military effectives for the Triple Alliance is affected unfavorably by the fact that Italy will for years to come have considerable forces tied down in Libya and that the complete and timely deployment of the military strength of the [Italian] Kingdom for the early decisive battles in a Triple Alliance war will encounter great obstacles even when that military strength is placed unreservedly at the service of the common cause."[18] Despite the unfavorable military balance to Austria-Hungary and Germany, the trends for the next few years did not inspire confidence either: by 1918 the Entente would add fifteen and a half divisions to their armed forces while the armies of the Central Powers would not expand at all. This memorandum makes clear Conrad's somber assessment of the heavy military odds facing the Monarchy if the conflict could not be confined to an armed struggle with Serbia.

Yet this gloomy assessment of the strategic balance did not deter Conrad from continuing to press for a war with Serbia. That streak of fatalism, so so readily apparent from Conrad's statements and writings, is nowhere more evident than in these deliberations among Habsburg decision makers during the July Crisis. Conrad simply would not relent in urging war. On July 5, during a rambling discussion with Kaiser Franz Joseph at the Schönbrunn palace, Conrad again asserted his view that war with Serbia was inevitable. While Franz Joseph agreed that a conflict with Serbia appeared imminent, he also thought that this meant a war with Russia. If Russia supported Serbia, Franz Joseph wanted to know how Conrad would deal with this contingency. Conrad answered that Germany would protect the Monarchy's rear from a Russian attack. Franz Joseph cautioned Conrad that Austria-Hungary could not count on Germany's unconditional support in the approaching confrontation with Serbia. It was Conrad's impression from this meeting that Franz Joseph was deferring his decision for war until he received assurances from Germany. The discussion became more heated when Conrad proposed that a state of martial law immediately be declared to prevent Serbian-sponsored terrorist attacks from disrupting mobilization. Franz Joseph adamantly refused to sanction this step; only after the proclamation of mobilization would martial law be declared.[19]

The next day, July 6, Conrad had another meeting with Berchtold that also included Count Johann Forgach, under-secretary of state at the foreign ministry. Conrad pushed for an answer from Berlin about whether Germany intended to support an immediate attack on Serbia. Forgach was optimistic of Germany's support, "first because of its alliance obligations, and second, it concerns Germany's existence as well." They agreed that, if German decision makers backed Austria-Hungary, Franz Joseph would consent to war. When Berchtold suggested that the Monarchy undertake a trial mobilization as a demonstration against Serbia, Conrad strongly disagreed. Conrad insisted on carrying out the complete mobilization under Case B. Berchtold told Conrad that Count István Tisza, the Hungarian prime minister, opposed going to war because he feared Russia's military intervention and a Romanian invasion of Transylvania. Berchtold wanted to know Conrad's view of the steps Russia might take in response to the Monarchy's mobilization against Serbia. Conrad replied that they needed to do nothing immediately. If Russia undertook threatening military moves, however, the Monarchy would need to mobilize and bring to war strength the three corps in Galicia. This military measure would provide a covering force in Galicia against a Russian preemptive attack. From this exchange, it clearly seems that Conrad envisioned the campaign against Serbia would be completed before Russia would make effective military moves against the Monarchy. Berchtold told Conrad that Berlin would want to know the Monarchy's war aims in a conflict with Serbia. Conrad replied: "Tell them, we do not know ourselves."[20] This episode illustrates the slipshod decision making of the Monarchy's leaders. Not able to agree about the Monarchy's political aims, they nonetheless plunged ahead. Instead of precise political aims, the objective became the military goal of destroying the Serbian army and occupying Belgrade. The Monarchy's leaders, then, waited for word from Berlin. Their decision to take action depended on the response of Germany's leaders.

GERMANY'S BLANK CHECK

Emotions in Berlin also ran high after the news of Franz Ferdinand's assassination, mirroring Tschirschky's observations on Vienna. Chancellor Bethmann Hollweg declared that Serbia had to bear the blame of an "undeniable moral co-responsibility."[21] Kaiser Wilhelm was deeply shocked by the death of Franz Ferdinand and his wife. The German emperor had gone to great lengths to cultivate a personal bond with the heir apparent, and Wilhelm appears to have developed a close, if paternal, relationship with Franz Ferdinand.[22] The importance of this personal bond must be kept in mind in understanding Wilhelm's initial emotional reaction to Franz Ferdinand's assassination. Like Franz Ferdinand, Wilhelm had worked to avoid war during the previous Balkan crisis. The loss of his friend, however, moved Wilhelm (at least during the initial stages of the crisis) into the camp of those who wanted to punish Serbia. Wilhelm's marginal comments on a memo from Tschirschky underscore his anger: "The Serbs must be disposed of, and right soon!" He supported action against Serbia even if this entailed the prospect of a confrontation with the Entente powers as well. Wilhelm thought that Serbia "had stained itself by an assassination." Consequently, Serbia would be diplomatically isolated if Vienna acted quickly in forcing a confrontation. "The Tsar would not in this case place himself on the side of regicides. Besides that, Russia and France were not prepared for war."[23] In Wilhelm's view, then, the terrorist attack against the Monarchy called for action against Serbia, and the international scene favored prompt, hard-line measures by Vienna.

Chancellor Bethmann Hollweg had his own reasons for wanting to encourage Vienna to adopt a hard line against Serbia. For Bethmann Hollweg, a confrontation between Austria-Hungary and Serbia provided an opportunity to improve Germany's diplomatic and strategic position. First, German support for Austria-Hungary would more firmly cement Vienna to the alliance with Germany. "If war comes from the east," Bethmann Hollweg remarked, "so that we have to fight for Austria-Hungary and not Austria-Hungary for us, we have a chance of winning."[24] Second, quick military action against Serbia might revitalize Austria-Hungary. Third, Serbia's defeat would strengthen Germany's position in the Balkans. Serbia would be reduced in territorial extent and military strength. Meanwhile, Bulgaria would jump on the Central Powers' bandwagon in the dismemberment of Serbia. Fourth, Italy and Romania would be less likely to defect from the Triple Alliance. These states would want to stay on the German bandwagon. Fifth, this confrontation might provide a way to split the Entente powers. This brinkmanship diplomacy carried the grave risk of war between the great powers. Yet Bethmann Hollweg hoped to exploit the very fear of war with Germany to break apart the Entente. Was Britain, for example, likely to underwrite Russia's Balkan ambitions and let itself be dragged into war with Germany? German decision makers did not think this contingency was likely.[25]

Finally, the German military leadership did not shrink from the prospect of war. Germany's chief of staff, Helmuth von Moltke, initially did not expect that the assassination would lead to war, so he did not bother to return from vacation taking the waters at Karlsbad. If war did occur, however, Moltke thought the moment opportune. Moltke's deputy, General von Waldersee, was even of the opinion "that they would regard it with favor if war were to come about now."[26]

In their meetings with Hoyos, Germany's leaders made clear their support of the Monarchy. Indeed, they pressed Vienna to take immediate action. Berlin made an important mistake, however: it had provided the green light for Austria-Hungary's action, but it did not have a precise picture of what Vienna's aims were or what action it intended to take. Germany's leaders could not have a clear picture of Vienna's goals because Habsburg decision makers did not even know what they aimed to do. Conrad's military operations plan to defeat the Serbian army in battle and overrun most of Serbia's territory was the closest thing that Austria-Hungary had to political direction for the war. This stance was clearly inadequate because it did not address the long-term relationship of Serbia to the Habsburg Monarchy. Once Austria-Hungary had been propelled toward war, however, its momentum would be difficult to stop if Berlin subsequently wanted to set limits on the actions of Vienna. Germany had committed itself to Austria-Hungary's drastic course of action without getting control over Vienna's management of the confrontation. Bethmann Hollweg's diplomacy of brinkmanship thus carried the risk of breaking apart the alliance with Austria-Hungary if Germany attempted to curb Vienna's actions.

VIENNA'S WAR DECISION

Count Hoyos returned to Vienna on the morning of July 7, and immediately reported to Berchtold that Berlin supported the Monarchy's proposed showdown with Serbia. Berchtold quickly relayed the findings of Hoyos to Conrad: "Germany will stand by our side unconditionally, even if our actions against Serbia should cause a great war. Germany urges us to attack." Berlin had issued the celebrated "blank check." Certain that war could not be long delayed, Conrad convinced the Archduke Friedrich, the commander-in-chief in case of war,[27] to postpone a scheduled trip to Hamburg. Soon afterwards, he spoke with Colonel Metzger, chief of the Operations Bureau, about mobilization measures. A decision on mobilization would have to wait until a council of the joint ministers met later that afternoon to discuss the policy options open to them.[28]

Now that Germany's support could be counted upon and German decision makers wanted Austria-Hungary to move quickly, Franz Joseph agreed to war with Serbia. Germany's support, however, did not resolve all the differences among Habsburg decision makers about the approaching showdown with Serbia. Franz Joseph remained worried that unrest within the Monarchy might take place. In particular, he thought trouble might arise in Hungary. Like Berchtold, Franz Joseph wanted to ensure popular support for a war with Serbia.[29] Nonetheless, Franz Joseph largely agreed with those advocating war. The aged emperor-king, the living embodiment of the Monarchy's stability and cohesion, might have done more to temper the demands made by his ministers and generals for a preventive war. Deeply upset by his nephew's death, Franz Joseph accepted the arguments made about the necessity for war. Since Germany's support was forthcoming and public opinion remained loyal, he did not inject any note of caution into the proceedings of his government's decision for war. As in 1859 and 1866, Franz Joseph proved all too ready to resort to force in an attempt to uphold the Monarchy's international position. His misjudgment, despite his long years of experience, was to have tragic consequences for his dynasty and country.[30]

Meanwhile, in Hungary, Tisza opposed war, and getting his agreement to a policy of confronting Serbia was essential to preserving political unity within the Monarchy. Tisza feared that Russia and Romania might enter the war and that the Romanian population in Transylvania would rise in rebellion against the domination of the Hungarians. He requested and received assurances from Conrad that the army was prepared to put down any insurrection that might occur within Transylvania.[31] He also wanted to be certain of Germany's support for the Monarchy in case of a confrontation and war with Russia.

Even with assurances of German support, Tisza wanted to avoid war, and he objected to taking immediate military action against Serbia. He told the German ambassador: the Monarchy's leaders "must proceed 'like gentlemen.' " When Wilhelm read Tisza's comments in the report from his ambassador, he wrote in the margin: "To act like 'gentlemen' to murderers, after what happened! Idiocy!"[32] Tisza argued that the Monarchy must present Belgrade with an ultimatum before undertaking military action. The ultimatum should attempt to humiliate Serbia and prevent future Serbian efforts to undermine Habsburg rule over the Slavs within Austria-Hungary. Only as a last resort should the Monarchy go to war with Serbia.

Finally, Tisza categorically rejected any notion of annexing territory from Serbia. By denying any interest in seizing Serbian territory, Tisza thought Russia might stay out of a Balkan conflict. Until the Hungarian prime minister's opposition was overcome, the Monarchy could not take military action.[33]

On July 7, during these critical deliberations, the government called in Conrad to explain the details of his deployment plans. The ministers asked if the Monarchy could mobilize initially only against Serbia and then later, if Russian intervention seemed imminent, against Russia. Conrad explained this could be done. He needed to know, however, by the fifth day of mobilization whether Russia planned to intervene so that the "B"-Staffel could deploy to Galicia and not Serbia.[34]

At a meeting on the evening of July 8, Conrad held further discussions with Berchtold and Baron Stephen Burian, the Hungarian minister in Vienna, Baron Karl von Macchio, an official from the foreign ministry, Count Forgach, and Count Hoyos. The meeting discussed the list of demands that Austria-Hungary would present in the ultimatum. It was also decided that the ultimatum would demand a reply within 24 or 48 hours.

Those attending the meeting agreed that Serbia would reject the demands made by Austria-Hungary. On the expiration of the time limit, they intended to order mobilization, and war would immediately follow. Conrad's determination to crush Serbia came across most clearly when Berchtold asked him what should the Monarchy do if the Serbian government capitulated to the demands of the ultimatum and offered no resistance. "Then we invade," Conrad told Berchtold. "Then Serbia remains occupied until the cost of the war is paid." Conrad argued that the goal of this war must be the destruction of Serbia's army and a heavy indemnity; the occupation of territory would not suffice to diminish the Serbian threat to the Monarchy. These deliberations show that the Monarchy's decision makers had no clear intentions about postwar territorial boundaries. In the short run, their goal consisted of humiliating Serbia and removing it as a military threat.[35]

In his desire to attack Serbia, Conrad did not even want to wait until the investigation of the assassination was completed before sending the ultimatum.[36] It would take at least two weeks before the investigation completed a report; meanwhile, Conrad feared if the Monarchy's enemies got wind of its plan to force a showdown with Serbia, they would use this time to prepare themselves for war. Berchtold suggested the deception scheme that both Conrad and Krobatin go on leave "to keep up the appearance that nothing is going on." Conrad repeated his view that diplomatic steps should be undertaken to ward off Romania's intervention against the Monarchy and discover Russia's intentions. Conrad wanted to find out at the earliest opportunity whether the Monarchy would also find itself at war with Russia. "If Russia orders a general mobilization," Conrad explained, "then the moment has come for us as well to declare mobilization against Russia." Berchtold insisted that no steps be taken that can "betray us; nothing at all must be done that attracts attention."[37] At a subsequent meeting on July 12, Conrad and Krobatin agreed to go away on vacation until July 22.[38]

This deception scheme was considered necessary to forestall military preparations by Serbia and Russia, and give the strategic initiative to the Monarchy in a confrontation. Conrad particularly wanted to prevent Serbia from mobilizing and deploying its army along the Monarchy's frontiers before Habsburg forces could concentrate. The chances for a rapid defeat of Serbia would increase if Habsburg forces could overcome the various river barriers along the frontiers before Serbian troops strengthened their defenses.[39]

Before departing on leave to the Tyrol, Conrad sent Berchtold a memorandum that contained his understanding of the decisions reached during the preceding two weeks.

For me, in my capacity as Chief of the General Staff, I am concerned only with the precise formulation of the decision in consideration, whether aiming directly at the outbreak of war with Serbia or only contending with the possibility of war.

The diplomatic handling of either alternative lies, of course, outside my province; however, I must again point out, as I explained verbally to Your Excellency with your complete approval, that in the diplomatic field everything must be avoided in the nature of protracted or piecemeal diplomatic action that would afford our adversary time for military measures and place us at a military disadvantage—that is disadvantage in general and more especially opposite Serbia and Montenegro.

In that sense everything should be avoided that would prematurely alarm our adversary and lead him to take countermeasures; in all respects a peaceable appearance should be displayed.

But once the decision to act has been taken, military considerations demand that it must be carried out in a single move with a short-term ultimatum, which if rejected, should be followed immediately by the mobilization order.[40]

Having reiterated his views, Conrad went on leave to the Tyrol on July 14.

While Conrad was away, the investigation of the assassination completed its report. Habsburg decision makers entrusted the investigation of Belgrade's complicity with the assassination to Dr. Friedrich von Wiesner, legal counselor to the foreign ministry. On July 10, Wiesner traveled to Sarajevo to examine the evidence on the assassination compiled by the civil and military authorities. Three days later, he reported his findings. To the chagrin of the Monarchy's decision makers, the investigation could produce no concrete proof of Belgrade's complicity with the assassination. Wiesner even considered the evidence showed "that such a conspiracy is out of the question." Thus, Habsburg investigators did not discover the links between the conspirators in Sarajevo and Dimitrijević, head of Serbian military intelligence and the mastermind of the plot to kill Franz Ferdinand. Although he lacked solid evidence to prove a conspiracy involving the Serbian government, Wiesner did conclude that the conspirators received arms from across the frontier. If Vienna intended to confront Belgrade, he recommended that the Monarchy make three principal demands. First, Austria-Hungary should insist on stricter policing by the Serbian government of their side of the frontier to prevent the smuggling of weapons across the border. Second, Belgrade should dismiss Serbian customs and police officials responsible for controlling Serbia's frontier with Bosnia. Third, Vienna should demand the arrest of known conspirators in the assassination living in Serbia.[41]

The findings and recommendations of the Wiesner investigation produced a strong reaction from the Monarchy's military leaders. From Sarajevo, General Potiorek, the governor of Bosnia, strongly disagreed with the investigation's conclusions. After seeing the report Wiesner intended to send to Vienna, Potiorek wrote Conrad saying that a great body of evidence existed showing "many Serbian officers on the active list and persons in high military positions played a leading part in these treacherous machinations." Of course, Potiorek admitted that a group of army officers, no matter how highly placed, was different from the civilian political leadership. He argued, however, that this group of officers was a "parallel military government." Furthermore, these Serbian officers could not possibly act "without at least the knowledge, if not encouragement, of the official Serbian government." He concluded by saying that the opportunity should not be lost "to destroy with a forceful hand the entire instrument of these plots, especially the Serbian army."[42] As his earlier statements show, Conrad completely agreed with Potiorek's assessment. There was general agreement within the army's leadership that the Monarchy's international position could only be restored by military operations. Specifically, the defeat of Serbia's army was the only path to providing for the Monarchy's security in the Balkans. As long as important factions in the Serbian army remained committed to using terrorism to promote a greater Serbia, the danger would not disappear. It is understandable that Austria-Hungary's military leaders concluded only the defeat and humiliation of the Serbian army would bring respite from Serbia's irredentism. After all, the savagery of the 1903 coup against the Serbian royal family and the actions of Dimitrijević in ordering the assassination of Franz Ferdinand show the ruthlessness displayed by nationalist extremists within Serbia's military. There could be no guarantee that, even if Pašić's government accepted Vienna's demands, the Serbian military might not continue to promote terrorism against Austria-Hungary. Berchtold concluded that Austria-Hungary's "situation must become more precarious as time goes on." If Austria-Hungary did not move against Serbian terrorism in 1914, "it would face another attack [by] Serbia in much more unfavorable conditions."[43]

Despite the inconclusiveness of Wiesner's report, the Monarchy's military leaders need not have feared that this opportunity for a confrontation with Serbia would be allowed to slip past. On July 14 Berchtold had finally worn down Tisza's resistance and gained his approval for war with Serbia. Berchtold had met all of Tisza's principal preconditions for confronting Serbia: namely, the Monarchy would first present Belgrade with an ultimatum before taking military action, the certain support of Germany in case of Russia's intervention, and a promise not to annex Serbian territory. Although giving his support to Berchtold, the Hungarian prime minister continued to hope that Serbia's humiliation and subordination could take place without resorting to war. For his part, Berchtold misled Tisza, encouraging the Hungarian leader to think that a war was still not inevitable.[44] In agreeing to war with Serbia, Tisza was strongly influenced by Berlin's support for the Monarchy. Germany's leaders expected Tisza to support Berchtold's confrontation with Serbia. Without this pressure from Berlin, Tisza might never have sanctioned war. In that circumstance, Franz Joseph would also probably balk at forcing a showdown. Tisza would later justify his decision by saying: "The noose was already tied around our neck. If we did not cut it, they would have strangled us later on. We could not have acted differently."[45] With Tisza won over, Berchtold no longer faced any serious opposition to a policy of provoking a war with Serbia.

While they had reached a consensus on foreign policy, Habsburg decision makers still faced the extraordinarily difficult task of orchestrating the confrontation with Serbia. In particular, they faced the difficult task of avoiding Russia's military intervention. This task required the highest diplomatic skills, a careful coordination of foreign policy initiatives and military moves, and an acute sense of political timing. It also required the ability to create policy options that maintained the diplomatic initiative for the Monarchy and attained the political goal of humiliating Serbia. The Monarchy's decision makers, however, lacked the skills required to master the diplomatic situation. Instead of exploiting opportunities to create options that furthered their political goals, they limited their policy choices and lost the initiative in the diplomatic contest. Their policy of brinkmanship degenerated into a crude power grab that spurred opposition from the other great powers.

One major problem confronting Habsburg decision makers was the coordination of their diplomatic offensive with the deployment of military forces against Serbia. The partial mobilization and deployment of forces against Serbia, or the so-called Case B, required fifteen days to complete. Until deployment was completed, Conrad remained adamant that the Monarchy could not carry out offensive operations. Berchtold's step-by-step diplomacy, however, entailed waiting until after Belgrade rejected the Monarchy's ultimatum before proclaiming mobilization. Thus, a period of over two weeks would intervene before the Monarchy could take military action against Serbia. During this time, Russia could deploy its armies in an attempt to forestall any Habsburg offensive against Serbia. Berchtold thought he could overcome this problem by immediately declaring war on Serbia after the expiration of the ultimatum. As events would show, this step was no real solution, and it only hobbled diplomatic efforts at keeping Russia from ordering mobilization. Perhaps Berchtold should have followed Conrad's advice and ordered a limited military deployment against Serbia in the immediate aftermath of Franz Ferdinand's murder. The deception scheme concocted by Berchtold utterly failed to lull Serbia and Russia into thinking that the Monarchy intended to take no further action. Because of maneuvers, which was the main reason for Franz Ferdinand's visit to Bosnia, the Monarchy already had two corps at full strength along Serbia's border. Mobilization of other neighboring corps could have occurred as well, holding them ready for deployment and shortening the time required for their eventual movement to the frontier. Of course, this step would have meant gaining Tisza's approval for these actions—not an easy task. If these steps were presented as a defensive measure, however, perhaps Tisza might have gone along. Clearly, Berchtold's inadequate grasp of the mechanics of mobilization and deployment prevented him from understanding the need for a more artful diplomacy. His diplomacy did not take into account sufficiently the time required to concentrate forces for military action. There was, then, a clear lack of coherence between the Monarchy's diplomacy and its military planning. Once Serbia rejected the ultimatum and Vienna declared war, the Monarchy's diplomacy lost much of its flexibility, and the initiative in the crisis passed to Saint Petersburg.

NOTES

1. The two standard accounts in English are Joachim Remak, *Sarajevo* (New York: Criterion Books, 1959), and Vladimir Dedijer, *The Road to Sarajevo* (New York: Simon and Schuster, 1966). These two studies supersede the earlier, anti-Habsburg account by R. W. Seton-Watson, *Sarajevo* (London: Hutchinson, 1925). Of course, because of the inadequate documentation on Belgrade's part in the assassination, none of these accounts can be considered definitive. On the difficulties of doing research on this topic in Belgrade, see the remarks of Professor Vaso Cubrilovic in Luigi Albertini, *The Origins of the War of 1914*, vol. 2, *The Crisis of July 1914* (London: Oxford University Press, 1953), 110.

2. Vladimir Dedijer, "Sarajevo Fifty Years After," *Foreign Affairs*, 42, 4 (1964): 569.

3. Tsar Nicholas told the British ambassador that the great powers must prepare for the coming partition of the Habsburg Monarchy. See *B.D.*, ix, part 2, no. 849, 690.

4. Imanuel Geiss, ed., *July 1914: The Outbreak of the First World War, Selected Documents* (New York: W. W. Norton, 1967), 64–65.

5. Vladimir Dedijer, "The Assassination of the Archduke Franz Ferdinand," *History of the First World War*, 1, (1): 8.

6. *AMD*, iv, 17. Conrad remained convinced to the end of his life of Belgrade's complicity in the assassination and that the Monarchy had no "other answer, no other solution, than *war against Serbia.*" See Conrad, *Private Aufzeichnungen*, Kurt Peball, ed. (Vienna: Amalthea-Verlag, 1977), 66.

7. Gina Conrad von Hötzendorf, *Mein Leben mit Conrad von Hötzendorf* (Graz: Verlag Styria, 1963), 558.

8. *AMD*, iv, 30.

9. On Austria-Hungary's decision making during the July Crisis, see Samuel R. Williamson, Jr., *Austria-Hungary and the Origins of the First World War* (New York: St. Martin's Press, 1991), 190–216.

10. *AMD*, iv, 33–34.

11. Bethmann Hollweg advised Wilhelm not to attend Franz Ferdinand's funeral for security reasons. Given the laxness of Habsburg security arrangements in Sarajevo, it is plain to see why Germany's leaders felt uneasy about Wilhelm's safety. See Konrad H. Jarausch, *The Enigmatic Chancellor: Bethmann Hollweg and the Hubris of Imperial Germany* (New Haven, Conn.: Yale University Press, 1973), 153.

12. Hugo Hantsch, *Leopold Graf Berchtold: Grandseigneur und Staatsmann* (Graz: Verlag Styria, 1963), 558.

13. See Williamson, *Austria-Hungary and the Origins of the First World War*, 49–50. Conrad married Gina in 1915 and scandalized much of Habsburg society by bringing her to live with him at the army's wartime headquarters in Teschen.

14. *AMD*, iv, 72.

15. Hantsch, *Berchtold*, 558–59.

16. *AMD*, iv, 34.

17. *ÖU*, viii, 9,976; Conrad's reply, Ibid., 9,995.

18. On the importance of Italy as a military factor during the July Crisis, see Michael Palumbo, "German-Italian Military Relations on the Eve of World War I," *Central European History*, 12, 4 (1979): 343–71. Of course, Italy remained neutral at the outbreak of war.

19. *AMD*, iv, 36–38. Conrad feared that Serbs living within the Monarchy would carry out acts of sabotage—blowing up bridges and railway lines—to disrupt the deployment of Habsburg forces to the frontiers.

20. Ibid., iv, 39–40.

21. Jarausch, *Enigmatic Chancellor*, 153.

22. Robert A. Kann, "Emperor William II and Archduke Francis Ferdinand in Their Correspondence," *The American Historical Review*, 57, 2 (1952): 323–51.

23. Albertini, *Origins*, ii, 142.

24. Konrad Jarausch, "The Illusion of Limited War: Chancellor Bethmann Hollweg's Calculated Risk, July 1914," *Central European History*, 2 (1969): 58.

25. On Bethmann Hollweg's diplomacy, see Jarausch, *Enigmatic Chancellor*, 148–84; and Fritz Stern, "Bethmann Hollweg and the War: The Limits of Responsibility," in *The Responsibility of Power*, ed. Leonard Krieger and Fritz Stern, (Garden City, N.Y.: Doubleday, 1967), 252–68.

26. Albertini, *Origins*, ii, 138.

27. In case of war, a nominal commander-in-chief had to be named, although Conrad would retain actual control over the direction of operations. Until his death, Franz Ferdinand was the prospective commander-in-chief in case of war. It was decided that the new heir apparent, the Archduke Karl, could not be given this responsibility because of his lack of military experience. Instead, the Archduke Friedrich was named to the position. On these issues of command in wartime, see *AMD*, iv, 107–8.

28. Ibid., iv, 42.

29. Albertini, *Origins*, ii, 171–73.

30. A psychological explanation for the fatalistic attitude of Habsburg decision makers during the July Crisis is offered by William Jannen, Jr., "The Austro-Hungarian Decision for War in July 1914," in *Essays on World War I: Origins and Prisoners of War*, ed. Samuel R. Williamson, Jr. and Peter Pastor (New York: Social Science Monographs, Brooklyn College Press, 1983), 55–81.

31. *AMD*, iv, 70.

32. Gabor Vermes, *István Tisza: The Liberal Vision and Conservative Statecraft of a Magyar Nationalist* (New York: East European Monographs, Columbia University Press, 1985), 227.

33. Norman Stone, "Hungary and the Crisis of July 1914," *Journal of Contemporary History*, 1, 3 (1966): 153–70.

34. *AMD*, iv, 53–54.

35. Ibid., 61–62.

36. Habsburg policy makers also decided that it was not prudent to send an ultimatum to Serbia while French President Poincaré was on a state visit to Russia. The ultimatum, then, would be held until July 23, after Poincaré's departure. See *AMD*, iv, 72.

37. Ibid., iv, 61–62.

38. Ibid., 72. Kaiser Wilhelm thought this deception scheme childish. See his marginal comment on a dispatch from Tschirschky to Jagow, 10 July 1914, *D.D.*, 29.

39. The bulk of the Serbian army's active strength was then deployed in the south of the Serbian kingdom, in the territories acquired during the Balkan wars of 1912–1913, known as Macedonia. The Habsburg general staff calculated that six days would be required to transfer these forces to the Danube front. On the movements of Serbian troops during the July Crisis, see *AMD*, iv, 70, 88.

40. Ibid., iv, 78.

41. *ÖU*, viii, 10,252–53.

42. *AMD*, iv, 82–85.

43. Bernadotte E. Schmitt, *The Coming of the War: 1914*, vol. 2 (New York: Charles Scribner's Sons, 1930), 18.

44. On Tisza's reluctance to begin a war with Serbia, see Albertini, *Origins*, ii, 178. The Austrian prime minister Stürgkh recalled: "Tisza was the only one against war, but we finally dragged him along too." Quoted in Eduard März, *Austrian Banking and Financial Policy: Creditanstalt at a Turning Point, 1913–1923*, trans. Charles Kessler (London: Weidenfeld and Nicolson, 1984), 106, n. 37.

45. Vermes, *István Tisza*, 231.

Chapter 5

Russia's Decision for War

The Habsburg Monarchy's decision makers realized that their planned action against Serbia carried with it a great risk of Russian military intervention. "Russia will never accept it," Franz Joseph predicted. "There will be a big war."[1] Nonetheless, Austria-Hungary's leaders intended to start a war with Serbia. "In resolving to deal firmly with Serbia," Berchtold began an instruction to Count Friedrich Szapary, the Monarchy's ambassador in Saint Petersburg, "we are of course aware of the possibility of a collision with Russia." This consideration, Berchtold continued, could not divert the Monarchy from action against Serbia, because Russia's patronage of Belgrade's expansionist policies represented a grave threat to Austria-Hungary.[2] Berchtold hoped that Russia would not intervene, and he possessed at least four good reasons to buttress this hope. First, Austria-Hungary was only undertaking this extreme action because of an act of state-sponsored terrorism. Second, Vienna intended no major territorial revisions in the Balkans. Third, he thought Serbia could be defeated quickly. Fourth, Germany's diplomatic support would act as a deterrent to aggressive Russian action. As the crisis unfolded, however, none of these assumptions proved correct, and Russia and Austria-Hungary were set on a clear collision course.

To Russian decision makers, Vienna's actions were a provocation that threatened Russia's prestige in the Balkans and its interest in the Turkish straits. The humiliation of Serbia and its conversion to a satellite of Austria-Hungary would overturn Russia's position in the Balkans.[3] Moreover, Vienna's evidence of Belgrade's complicity in the assassination was very weak. The investigation by Habsburg authorities had turned up precious little concrete proof of the Serbian government's direct involvement in the murder. This lack of any solid evidence for a conspiracy meant that Russia's foreign minister Sergei Sazonov had no "golden bridge," enabling him to back down from supporting Serbia. The lack of any conclusive evidence linking the Serbian government to the assassination thus made Austria-Hungary's actions look like a provocation to Russia. Finally, Berlin's apparent support for Austria-Hungary's actions was viewed as another attempt to humiliate Russia. Russia's leaders could not afford a repeat of the Bosnian Crisis of 1908–1909. Russia, then, was facing a trial of strength not only with Austria-Hungary but with Germany as well. Unlike 1909, Russia was in a military and domestic political position where it could take up the challenge being offered by Vienna and Berlin.[4] It was clear to Russian decision makers that a confrontation with Austria-Hungary entailed running the high risk of conflict with Germany. On July 24, upon learning of the terms of Vienna's ultimatum to Serbia, Russia's foreign minister Sazonov exclaimed: "C'est la guerre européenne!"[5] Despite the increased risk of general war, Russia's leaders decided that they must make a strong and immediate response to prevent Austria-Hungary from achieving a fait accompli and overrunning Serbia. This response included coercive military movements against Austria-Hungary. The confrontation with Austria-Hungary during the Balkan wars of 1912–1913 and the July Crisis show Russian policy makers saw military measures as an integral part of their diplomacy. While this heavy-handed use of military measures did not produce a conflict in 1912, it was to have the most unfortunate of consequences during the summer of 1914.

In response to Vienna's ultimatum to Serbia, Sazonov moved quickly during July 24 to formulate Russia's foreign policy stance. First, he telephoned the news to the Tsar, who responded laconically: "This is disturbing." Throughout the crisis, Nicholas proved more reluctant than his ministers and generals to begin taking military steps against Austria-Hungary and Germany. Yet, he agreed with them that Russia could not stand back while Austria-Hungary attacked Serbia. Although he wanted to avoid conflict with Germany, Nicholas would not accept a repeat of the 1909 humiliation.

Second, Sazonov met with the French ambassador Maurice de Paléologue and the British ambassador Sir George Buchanan. At his meeting with them, Sazonov received what he was looking for, namely diplomatic support from Russia's Entente partners. Paléologue provided a "blank check," promising France's support for Russia in its dispute with Austria-Hungary.[6] Buchanan reported on the meeting: "The French ambassador gave me to understand that France would not only give Russia strong diplomatic support, but would, if necessary, fulfill all obligations imposed on her by the alliance." Britain could do little, Buchanan contended, to restrain France and Russia. "From the French Ambassador's language," Buchanan reported, "it almost looked as if France and Russia were determined to make a strong stand even if we [that is, Britain] declined to join them."[7] Thus, Britain ran the risk of splitting its ententes with both France and Russia if it did not support Saint Petersburg in this confrontation with

Austria-Hungary.[8] The determination of France and Russia to confront the Central Powers came in part from the recent visit to Saint Petersburg by French President Raymond Poincaré and Prime Minister René Viviani. Their state visit highlighted the solidarity of the Dual Alliance and the growing military strength of Russia. The afterglow of this summit strengthened Russia's leaders in their resolve, since they could count on French support even if the confrontation resulted in war.[9] In the opinion of the Russian historian V. I. Bovykin, Russia's leaders "decided to take up a firm position in relation to Germany, only when they were fully convinced of the support of France and Great Britain."[10] Without guarantees of assistance from their Entente partners, Russia's leaders could not consider starting a war against Austria-Hungary and Germany.

Third, he called a meeting of Russia's council of ministers for the afternoon of July 24.[11] In this important meeting, Russia's leaders made the decision for war with Austria-Hungary and, if necessary, Germany. According to Baron M. Schilling, the head of the Russian Foreign Ministry's chancery, Sazonov "considered war unavoidable." He argued that Germany was attempting to humiliate Russia again, as it had done during the Bosnian crisis. Russia's historic support of the Slavic peoples of the Balkans would be discredited, and its imperial ambitions in the region at an end. If Saint Petersburg accepted this dictation, Russia would drop to the status of a second-class power. A. V. Krivoshein, the Russian minister for agriculture and perhaps the foremost figure in the government, argued that Russia was sufficiently recovered from the defeats of the Russo-Japanese War and revolutionary disturbances to consider war. Krivoshein went further in his assessment of the interrelationship of Russia's domestic political situation and foreign policy. The regime would face political turmoil at home, in his opinion, if it stood by and permitted Austria-Hungary to crush Serbia. Unrest might even come if it did not stand by Serbia. Krivoshein observed that "public and parliamentary opinion would fail to understand why, at this critical moment involving Russia's vital interests, the Imperial Government was reluctant to act boldly." Now the regime needed to fear more the domestic political consequences of inaction than risking a war with the Central Powers. David McDonald is certainly correct in arguing: "it is difficult to conceive of any Russian government that could have held back from action in support of Serbia in July 1914. Its domestic authority already severely compromised by deteriorating relations with the Duma, advancing social unrest, and disarray within its own ranks, in refusing to aid Serbia the Russian government would have severed its last link with civil society."[12] The government agreed that, from a domestic political point of view, Russia must resist the attempt by the Central Powers to defeat Serbia. Since France backed Russian action, there could be no excuse for backing down under pressure from Austria-Hungary and Germany.

In the debate, no powerful dissenting voice warned of the dangers of a European war. In the past, Stolypin and Kokovtsev had argued the necessity of avoiding war until Russia's society and economy could withstand the strain. Their caution had prevailed on previous occasions. But changes in the makeup of the Russian government from the preceding year were important in determining the outcome of the debate. Kokovtsev was no longer in power, and his voice cautioning moderation and the danger of war for Russia was not heard as it had been during the Balkan crisis. Although Russia's leaders in July 1914 understood that Russia was not a match for Germany, they saw no alternative. There were no doves in the government. To be sure, Nicholas took some time to convince. Although Nicholas was later to temporize over whether to order a general mobilization, he accepted the necessity of taking a hard line against Austria-Hungary, despite his fears of a war with Germany. By July 30, even the Tsar "agreed that under the existing circumstances it would be very dangerous not to make timely preparations for what was apparently an inevitable war."[13]

Fourth, Sazonov also called in Szapary and protested the ultimatum. Szapary reported to Vienna that the Russian foreign minister charged:

You mean to make war on Serbia. . . . You are setting fire to Europe. It is a great responsibility you are assuming, you will see the impression that it will make here and in London and Paris and perhaps elsewhere. It will be regarded as an unjustifiable aggression. . . . The monarchic ideal has got nothing to do with it. . . . The fact is you mean war and you have burnt your bridges. . . . One sees how peace loving you are, seeing that you set fire to Europe.[14]

Fifth, Sazonov encouraged Belgrade to resist the extreme demands put on it by the Monarchy's ultimatum. Although Sazonov did not provide an unconditional guarantee of support to Belgrade, he did promise Russian backing against any attempt by Austria-Hungary to crush Serbian independence. If Austria-Hungary attacked Serbia, however, Russia would militarily intervene.[15]

Finally, to provide muscle for his diplomacy, Sazonov summoned the chief of the Russian general staff, General Nikolai Yanushkevich, to find ways to exert military pressure on Austria-Hungary. Throughout the crisis, the use of military alerts, mobilization, and deployments against Austria-Hungary were never far removed from Sazonov's mind. As early as July 18, Sazonov was considering mobilization if Vienna forced a showdown with Serbia. On that day he told Britain's ambassador Buchanan "that anything in the nature of an Austrian ultimatum at Belgrade could not leave Russia indifferent, and that she might be forced to take some precautionary military measure."[16] Moreover, at the important meetings of the Council of Ministers held on July 24 and 25, Russia's policy makers sanctioned the immediate mobilization against Austria-Hungary.[17] Consequently, Russia was already undertaking important preparatory steps for mobilization and deployment by July 26.

Some scholars who have closely examined Russian actions during the July Crisis assert that Sazonov and the Russian military leadership committed a serious strategic mistake in resorting so quickly to mobilization against Austria-Hungary. After all, they argue, would not Russia's strategic position improve if Austria-Hungary got bogged down in a protracted struggle against Serbia? Once a substantial portion of Austria-Hungary's army was fighting in the Balkans, the military balance would tilt decisively in favor of Russia. A Russian attack into Galicia would then face fewer Habsburg forces. Yet Russia's leaders missed this opportunity to exploit Austria-Hungary's strategic predicament. In his account of the July Crisis, L.C.F. Turner condemns Sazonov and the Russian generals for failing "to grasp the immense diplomatic and military advantage conferred on them by the Austrian dilemma."[18]

This strategic assessment rests on the assumption that Serbia could withstand the initial attack by Austria-Hungary. Conrad intended to amass over twenty divisions in the Balkans, providing Austria-Hungary with a two-to-one numerical superiority over Serbia. Moreover, he planned to use this superiority for an early offensive onto Serbian soil. With three armies deployed on the Balkan front, Austria-Hungary possessed the forces to defeat the Serbian army in battle if it decided to stand and fight. Habsburg forces might then occupy Belgrade and most of the Serbian kingdom. To be sure, Serbia's army would no doubt give a good account of itself in fighting back an invasion. The Serbian army possessed good morale and combat leaders, was battle tested, and fought in rugged terrain. Yet Sazonov and Russia's military leadership could not assume that Conrad's planned offensive would fail. No matter how bravely the Serbs fought, Austria-Hungary's numerical superiority might prove too great to overcome. Austria-Hungary might win quickly, and then Russia's intervention might come too late. In effect, Russia would play the part that Berchtold and Conrad hoped it would: that is, stand aside and permit a local Balkan war between Austria-Hungary and Serbia to take place.

Other political and strategic factors shaped Sazonov's decision to force an early showdown with Austria-Hungary. For Sazonov, the use of military measures was not unusual. After all, both Austria-Hungary and Russia had undertaken partial mobilizations during the Balkan wars of 1912–1913. Both sides saw military demonstrations as a way of shaping the political outcome of those struggles and enhance their security. On that occasion, Russia's trial mobilization served as a not so subtle reminder to Habsburg decision makers that an attack on Serbia would also involve a military confrontation with Russia. Throughout the Balkan crisis, Vienna labored under this threat to the country's security. It was Sazonov's intention to

re-create this threat as a weapon of intimidation against Austria-Hungary—
to back up his diplomacy with force.[19]

Preparatory military measures also had an added strategic advantage: if
diplomatic efforts to prevent war failed, Russia's armies would at least be
ready to begin military operations. Ever mindful of the time it took to
deploy their armies to the frontier, Russia's military leaders were all too
willing to begin making military preparations. Sazonov's diplomacy thus
coincided with the requests of Russia's military leadership that mobilization and deployment start immediately. Russian military leaders called for
military preparations even though Austria-Hungary and Germany had not
undertaken any actions against Russia.[20] That Russia's leaders intended to
use military deployments as a weapon of intimidation is often lost sight of
in the debate among historians whether Russia needed to carry out a
general mobilization or whether it might have undertaken a more limited
deployment against only Austria-Hungary. This issue, however, is a red
herring. No matter how much Russian decision makers might have wanted
to fine tune their military preparations, there can be no disguising that their
actions greatly increased the risk of a general war. If Russia did not make
military preparations against Austria-Hungary and Germany, Vienna and
Berlin would get their way, and the conflict would have remained "localized" to the Balkans. Determined to prevent this from occurring, Russia's
leaders raised the stakes of the confrontation to include that of general war.
Thus, Sazonov's diplomacy of force was another important step toward a
European-wide conflagration. For the Russian government, war became
inevitable when Austria-Hungary rejected Belgrade's answer to the ultimatum and refused efforts to mediate the conflict.[21]

Of course, Sazonov's actions can be defended on the grounds that he did
not understand the fateful implications of his actions in triggering war.
After all, Russia's mobilization and deployment need not entail war; diplomacy could still settle the confrontation even though the armies of the great
powers were drawn up along the frontiers. During the Balkan crisis, the
mobilization and deployment of substantial Russian and Habsburg military forces along their common frontier in Galicia did not automatically
result in war. While these military measures complicated the diplomacy of
the crisis, they did not trigger war. In 1914, however, Russian military steps
would have a different result. What Sazonov did not fathom was that
Russia's actions might precipitate Germany's employment of the Schlieffen
Plan. German decision makers viewed Russia's diplomacy with great
alarm: it appeared to Berlin as a deception scheme to cloak a covert
deployment of Russian armies on the frontier, in preparation for a full-scale
offensive into Germany and Austria-Hungary. Russia's leaders might have
thought there was nothing incompatible with simultaneously continuing
negotiations and deploying armies toward the frontiers. The reality, however, was much different. Russia's military preparations and the initial

attempts to conceal them greatly shortened the amount of time available for a diplomatic settlement.

NOTES

1. G. P. Gooch, *History of Modern Europe, 1878–1919* (New York: Henry Holt, 1923), 536.

2. *ÖU*, viii, 721–24.

3. See, for example, Serge Sazonov, *Fateful Years, 1909–1916* (London: Jonathan Cape, 1928), 179.

4. On Russia's recovery from the Russo-Japanese War, see Norman Stone, *Europe Transformed, 1878–1919* (Cambridge: Harvard University Press, 1984), 197–254.

5. Baron M. F. Schilling, *How the War Began in 1914* (London: George Allen and Unwin, 1925), 28–29. Schilling's diary is an invaluable source for tracking Russian decision making during the crisis.

6. On France's diplomacy during the July Crisis and the important role played by Paléologue, see the study by John F. V. Keiger, *France and the Origins of the First World War* (New York: St. Martin's Press, 1983), 145–67.

7. *B.D.*, xi, 101.

8. On British diplomacy during the July Crisis, see the conflicting interpretations offered by Zara S. Steiner, *Britain and the Origins of the First World War* (New York: St. Martin's Press, 1977), 215–57; and Keith M. Wilson, *The Policy of the Entente: Essays on the Determinants of British Foreign Policy, 1904–1914* (Cambridge: Cambridge University Press, 1985), 135–47.

9. France's military leadership also encouraged Russia to take a firm stand in the crisis. They were particularly eager that Russia begin an early offensive into East Prussia. See L.C.F. Turner, *Origins of the First World War* (New York: Norton, 1970), 103–4.

10. V. I. Bovykin, "The Franco-Russian Alliance," 35.

11. On this pivotal meeting, see D.C.B. Lieven, *Russia and the Origins of the First World War* (New York: St. Martin's Press, 1983), 141–44.

12. David MacLaren McDonald, *United Government and Foreign Policy in Russia, 1900–1914* (Cambridge: Harvard University Press, 1992), 218. The Russian historian V. I. Bovykin's contention that Russia's "internal situation . . . exercised a very strong moderating influence on the directors of Russian foreign policy" does not seem borne out by this meeting. See Bovykin, "Franco-Russian Alliance," 35.

13. Schilling, *How the War Began*, 65–66.

14. Geiss, *Documents*, 174–75.

15. On Saint Petersburg's blank check to Belgrade, see Gale Stokes, "The Serbian Documents from 1914: A Preview," *Journal of Modern History*, 48, 3 (1976): on-demand supplement. In addition, see Albertini's analysis, *Origins*, ii, 350–72.

16. *B.D.*, xi, 60.

17. On these important deliberations of the Russian Council of Ministers, see the valuable study by Lieven, *Russia and the Origins of the First World War*, 139–51.

18. See Turner, *Origins of the First World War*, 92–93; Jack S. Levy, "Preferences, Constraints, and Choices in July 1914," *International Security* 15, 3 (1990/91): 254.

19. See Lieven, *Russia and the Origins of the First World War*, 147–49.

20. See William C. Fuller, Jr., *Strategy and Power in Russia, 1600–1914* (New York: The Free Press, 1992), 445–51.

21. On this point, see the convincing arguments made by Marc Trachtenberg, "The Coming of the First World War: A Reassessment," in *History and Strategy* (Princeton: Princeton University Press, 1991), 76–87.

Chapter 6

Vienna and Berlin Order General Mobilization

When Belgrade ordered mobilization on July 24, in response to the ultimatum delivered the day before, Conrad received permission to mobilize
against Serbia. The machinery began operating under Case B, with July 28
designated as the first day of mobilization: the Second Army, the Balkan
Group, and the III Corps headquartered in Graz received orders to mobilize.
The III Corps belonged to the "*A*"-*Staffel*, that is, it was intended for Galicia
in case of war and not for the Balkans. Austria-Hungary mobilized this
corps, Conrad explained in his memoirs, to guard against an attack by Italy
or to contain unrest in Bohemia. The real purpose behind the mobilization
of the III Corps, however, was that Conrad intended to use it against Serbia.[1]
Conrad's decision to use the III Corps in the Balkans, even though it might
be needed in Galicia, shows his determination to mass his forces for a
knockout blow against Serbia.

Since Austria-Hungary was initially massing its forces against only
Serbia, the question arose about what military steps the Monarchy could
take if Russia intervened. Earlier in the crisis, at the important July 7
meeting of the Monarchy's decision makers, Conrad had stated that he
needed to know within five days of the proclamation of mobilization
against Serbia whether Russia intended to intervene. After five days, the
"*B*"-*Staffel* would deploy to the Balkans and could not go to Galicia. The
first day of mobilization against Serbia under the provisions of Case B was
scheduled for July 28. Conrad thus needed to know Russia's intentions by
August 1. If Russia revealed her intentions to attack by that date, the
"*B*"-*Staffel* would go to Galicia under the provisions of Case Russia. Once
the "*B*"-*Staffel* started to move toward Serbia, however, it could not be
recalled and sent to Galicia, but would have to complete its deployment to
the Danube and only then could it be transported to Galicia from Serbia.

It did not take long before good intelligence began arriving that indicated Russia's intention to intervene militarily in support of Serbia. As we know, Russia began making preparations for mobilization as early as July 26, and within two days intelligence sources provided evidence of Russian military measures aimed at Austria-Hungary. Faced by the mounting evidence of Russian military preparations, Conrad even urged Berchtold on July 27 to secure Germany's diplomatic cooperation in deterring the deployment of Russian armies against the Monarchy. Without assurances of German support, the *"B"-Staffel* would deploy in Galicia. What was at stake, then, was the Monarchy's ability to undertake offensive operations against Serbia.

In response to Conrad's request, Berchtold wired the Monarchy's ambassador in Berlin, Count Ladislaus Szögyeny-Marich, the next day, asking that German intentions be made clear. Furthermore, Szögyeny was to alert German decision makers that Russian military deployments threatened not only the Monarchy but Germany's security as well. Consequently, the time was fast approaching when Berlin would be required to use "plain language" and threaten military countermeasures if Russia continued its deployments. Mindful of the Romanian army's potential military significance in drawing off Russian forces from the Monarchy's frontiers, Berchtold also wanted Germany to approach King Carol and secure Romania's diplomatic cooperation in dealing with Russia. Securing Romanian adherence to the Triple Alliance would improve the Monarchy's strategic position and perhaps even permit Conrad to continue with his planned attack on Serbia.

Any doubts about Russia's intentions were dispelled on the afternoon of July 29, when Count Nikolai Schebeko, the Russian ambassador in Vienna, told Tschirschky that Saint Petersburg had ordered mobilization of the Kiev, Moscow, Odessa, and Kazan military districts. Russia ordered this partial mobilization as a move against the Habsburg Monarchy. Tschirschky promptly sent Berlin a telegram with this news and told Berchtold of his conversation with the Russian ambassador. It also became clear by August 1 that Germany planned to order mobilization in response to Russia's military preparations.

Despite this evidence of an impending clash with Russia, Conrad permitted the *"B"-Staffel* to entrain for the Balkans "to achieve a swift and decisive success" over Serbia.[2] What led him to make this strategic mistake in deployment? Two principal explanations can be adduced. First, Conrad did not think that Russia's mobilization would necessarily lead to war. While Austria-Hungary needed to take precautionary countermeasures to avoid the development of a dangerous imbalance of forces along the Galician frontier, a clash of arms was not inevitable. Secondly, Conrad thought that Germany's diplomatic and military actions would force Russia to back down. Both assumptions proved false, but it should be noted that Conrad was not alone among Habsburg decision makers in deprecating the importance of Russia's actions. The Habsburg foreign ministry also played down the significance of Russia's threatening intervention. The foreign ministry's cavalier attitude toward Russia horrified the Austrian financier Rudolf Sieghart. When Sieghart warned Forgach that Russia's intervention was imminent, the foreign ministry's under-secretary replied, "with an indescribable mixture of indifference and hauteur, 'Well, let them.' "[3] Among Habsburg decision makers the view was widespread that the mere threat of German intervention would dissuade Russia from beginning a great-power war.

That Conrad did not think Russia would immediately enter the conflict is clear from his meetings with other Habsburg decision makers on July 29. Conrad told Berchtold that Russia's threatening military deployments required the Monarchy to undertake its own mobilization and countering deployments in Galicia. Conrad used blunt language: "If Russia mobilizes, we should also have to mobilize." Berchtold demurred from such a drastic step because of the cost of mobilizing the entire armed forces against Serbia and Russia. Conrad stressed, however, the military dangers of letting Russia gain a lead over Austria-Hungary in deploying forces along the Galician frontier. If Russia deployed its armies, and Austria-Hungary failed to take countermeasures, then "the road to Budapest and Vienna would lie open to the Russians." Conrad considered "it irresponsible to fold our arms and not carry out our own mobilization in view of what was already without doubt Russian mobilization."[4] Albertini alleges that Berchtold went along with Conrad's call for a general mobilization because the Habsburg foreign minister wanted to sabotage Germany's eleventh-hour attempts to prevent a great-power war.[5] This interpretation is highly speculative and unconvincing, and there is no need for such a Machiavellian explanation for Berchtold's actions. Russia's diplomatic representative in Vienna had openly admitted that his country was already mobilizing against Austria-Hungary. Russian military preparations had been progressing for almost a week. Given these Russian military steps, it is surely not surprising that Austria-Hungary would start taking measures to provide for its own security from attack.

It is important to emphasize that in Conrad's view competitive mobilizations and deployments by Russia and Austria-Hungary along the Galician frontier did not inevitably mean war. As long as Russia did "not touch us," Conrad argued, "we need not touch them either." His goal was to close any "window of vulnerability" that Russia might open by completing its deployment before Austria-Hungary. In Conrad's opinion, the deployment of the *"A"-Staffel*, or approximately 27 divisions, should deter Russia from using any of its forces for an offensive into the Monarchy. On the other hand, if deterrence failed and Russia attacked, the three Habsburg armies deployed in Galicia could fight a defensive battle along the San River, protecting Hungary and Moravia from invasion. This defense would also permit a concentration of three armies for a rapid campaign to overrun Serbia. As early as July 14, Conrad told general staff officers that Habsburg forces in Galicia would deploy in a defensive line along the San and Dneister rivers.[6] For Conrad, then, mobilization and deployment did not make war with Russia inevitable; the concentration of forces in Galicia was a precaution to guard the Monarchy against a Russian assault. It was Conrad's fear that the absence of a Habsburg mobilization, in response to Russia's military moves, might prompt a Russian attack. If Habsburg forces did not move rapidly into Galicia, Austria-Hungary's vulnerability might be too tempting for Russia not to exploit.

Conrad's views about the relationship between mobilization and the outbreak of war call into question some of the conclusions reached by recent studies on the so-called cult of the offensive.[7] No important military figure before 1914 was more vehement than Conrad in exhorting the merits of offensive operations. Nonetheless, Conrad did not blindly think that deployment made war inevitable or that its completion necessarily entailed undertaking the offensive. Conrad could envision mobilized and deployed armies cautiously watching each other across the frontier, with neither side striking first. What this episode highlights is the importance of political and strategic calculations in determining Conrad's decision about whether to carry out an offensive against Russia. In Conrad's case, the so-called cult of the offensive, derived from organizational imperatives, does not explain his military plans. Instead, Conrad's plans were shaped by his political aims and his assessment of the overall balance of military forces.

What was foremost in Conrad's mind was obtaining sufficient time to defeat Serbia before a Russian attack against the Monarchy. Conrad did not ignore Russia's military deployments against the Monarchy. He did not think, however, that this automatically would lead to a war with Russia. Moreover, Russia's deployment did not deter him from wanting to attack and overrun Serbia. Because he did not consider it immediately necessary to fight Russia, Conrad even intended to establish his headquarters with the Archduke Friedrich at a command center located in Kamenitza near Peterwardein in Hungary. From this location, he would direct operations against Serbia. Conrad told his staff that Austria-Hungary could probably count on a two-week period to attack Serbia before Russia was likely to intervene in the conflict.[8] On July 30, Conrad told Berchtold: "Who knows whether there will be war with Russia after all? The Russians might quite as well stand still expecting us to drop our plans against Serbia."[9]

As it turned out, Conrad committed a great blunder in deciding to send the "B"-Staffel to the Balkans in the face of Russian mobilization. This mistake greatly contributed to the heavy defeats suffered by Austria-Hungary during the opening months of the war. After the war, Conrad tried to blame his incorrect deployment on technical considerations.[10] This explanation, however, is patently untrue. An order recalling the "B"-Staffel only went out on August 5. The actual movement of the *"B"-Staffel* against Russia could only begin on August 19 when the rail lines to Galicia became free after the transportation of the *"A"-Staffel*. Some units of the *"B"-Staffel* (also known as the Second Army) had become involved in the fighting when they arrived on the Serbian front. Once this occurred, they could only be extricated with difficulty. Three divisions remained behind and were not moved at all to the Russian front. Conrad recalled the *"B"-Staffel* only after he learned from Moltke that the German Narew offensive would not take place. Conrad had counted on a German offensive threat to distract the Russians while Habsburg forces overran Serbia. By withdrawing the *"B"-Staffel* at such a late date, however, it arrived in Galicia only after the crucial opening battles had already been fought and lost. (Appendix II provides an overview of the movements of the Second Army during the July Crisis and the initial period of operations.)

In his history of the First World War, Winston Churchill explained the military significance of what happened: Conrad had "fooled away the power of the Second Army in both theatres." Once he had committed the Second Army to the Danube, there was little chance of bringing it back to Galicia in time to fight in the early battles. Conrad should have left the *"B"-Staffel* to win the victory over Serbia—a victory practically ensured by the Habsburg two-to-one superiority in numbers. "It was his paramount duty to make the Second Army fight somewhere at the crucial moment." Instead, the Second Army left the Balkans before it had a chance to win a victory over Serbia. Moreover, it arrived in Galicia only to take part in the debacle suffered in that theater at the hands of the Russians.[11] Conrad remained convinced throughout most of the crisis that the war was a conflict between Austria-Hungary and Serbia. It is only by keeping this perspective in mind that the movement of the *"B"-Staffel* to the Danube makes any sense. These wanderings of the *"B"-Staffel* thus support Joachim Remak's contention that the First World War started as the outbreak of the Third Balkan War.[12]

Could Conrad have despatched the *"B"-Staffel* to the Russian front instead of sending it against Serbia? Count Karl Kageneck, the German military attaché in Vienna, thought that this movement was possible as late as August 1. Kageneck lobbied Habsburg military planners, trying to convince them to move the *"B"-Staffel* to Galicia. In discussions with Colonel Christophori, who headed the operations section of Austria-Hungary's general staff dealing with war planning against Russia, Kageneck argued that Conrad should immediately countermand orders for the movement of the *"B"-Staffel* to the Balkans. Because most of the units making up the *"B"-Staffel* had not yet moved from their mobilization centers, Kageneck contended that they could deploy to Galicia before the movement of the *"A"-Staffel*. Thus, Austria-Hungary could carry out a concentration of these two echelons in Galicia, facilitating an early Habsburg offensive into Russian Poland. Christophori agreed with Kageneck's analysis of the strategic situation and the feasibility of his deployment plan.[13] That Kageneck's plan was feasible is supported by a study done by the Swiss military historian General Bela von Lengyel. In a careful analysis of the transportation problems standing in the way of this deployment scheme, Lengyel concludes that Austria-Hungary could have carried out an early movement of the "B"-Staffel to Galicia.[14]

Conrad did apparently ask his chief of the Railway Bureau Colonel Straub, on the evening of July 31, whether such a deployment was possible. Straub was aghast at the suggestion. Last-minute changes in the Monarchy's deployment, in Straub's opinion, would spell disaster. First, Straub maintained that the railway lines to Galicia were not prepared for the large-scale movement of troop transports. Second, portions of the "B"-Staffel had already moved to the Serbian frontier. Thus, a change in plans would disorganize units in the "B"-Staffel. Third, Straub feared that the hasty movement of the "B"-Staffel might delay the later deployment of the "A"-Staffel, disrupting the entire plan to deploy against Russia. Straub warned that "a catastrophe might occur" if they tried to carry out this change in plans.[15] Because of his meetings with the officers of the Railway Bureau, Conrad abandoned any notion of diverting the "B"-Staffel to the Russian theater of operations.

The movement of the "B"-Staffel to the Serbian frontier had important repercussions in Berlin during the crucial last days of July. The Kaiser and Bethmann Hollweg supported Vienna's hard line policy toward Belgrade, but wanted to keep the approaching conflict limited to a Balkan War between Austria-Hungary and Serbia. When it became apparent that Saint Petersburg was unlikely to permit this, Berlin's policy became one of moderating Vienna's demands and preventing war with Russia: the Kaiser's "hotline" messages to his cousin the Tsar—the famous Willi-Nicky correspondence—and his "Halt in Belgrade" scheme were attempts to mediate the crisis. On July 30, Bethmann Hollweg even went so far as to warn Vienna:

the refusal of all exchange of views with Saint Petersburg would be a grave error, since it would provoke armed intervention by Russia which it is, more than anything, to Austria-Hungary's interest to avoid.

We are of course ready to fulfill our duty as allies, but must decline to let ourselves be dragged by Vienna, wantonly and without regard to our advice, into a world conflagration.[16]

Berlin was now prepared to settle the dispute by opening negotiations.

But Germany's leaders also had to be prepared, in case these attempts to prevent war failed, to make sure that it entered the conflict politically united at home by having the support of the Social Democrats, the largest party in the Reichstag. This support could only be assured if Russia took the first overtly hostile act of mobilization.[17] Domestic political considerations required that the German public perceive war as a last resort, forced upon Germany by Russian military actions.

Moltke returned from his vacation in Karlsbad on July 26 to find the government making attempts to prevent war between Austria-Hungary and Russia. In Berlin, Moltke also found waiting for him intelligence reports on the extensive nature of the Russian military preparations.[18] With this information in front of him, Moltke composed on July 28 his famous memorandum, *"Zur Beurteilung der politischen Lage,"* which he presented to Bethmann the next day.[19] This memorandum is often cited as showing the undue influence of the military in Wilhelmine Germany's political affairs.[20] Fritz Fischer used this document to condemn the ethos of the Prussian-German state: "The system of the German constitution, Bismarck's heritage and even more the heritage of the spirit of the Prussian military monarchy, that is the institutions and the social factors, were more powerful elements than the insight or will of an individual."[21]

Yet Fischer and his epigones overstate their case: Moltke's assessment is not nearly so damning as they allege. Moltke began by stating the obvious—namely, there existed a very real chance of war breaking out between Austria-Hungary and Russia. Under the terms of the 1879 alliance, a Russian military attack against Austria-Hungary would constitute the *casus foederis*; Germany could not stand by in this conflict, but would have to mobilize as well. Furthermore, Moltke contended that Russia was attempting to deceive Germany about the extent of its military preparations. In Moltke's view, Saint Petersburg's protestations that Russia was not carrying out mobilization—only making "military preparations"—was a cunning deception to put the onus for mobilizing first on Austria-Hungary and Germany. Moltke thought that Russia had already decided on war because of the extent of its military buildup, and in retrospect he seems correct.[22]

It is even more remarkable that, in the face of the Russian military preparations, Moltke did not ask for an immediate mobilization by Germany. Moltke was much more moderate in this instance than the Prussian War Minister General Erich von Falkenhayn, who demanded an immediate military response to the Russian buildup.[23] Instead of mobilization, Moltke only wanted the Wilhelmstrasse to clarify the position of the Russian and French governments as to their "preparations." If they did not find out soon, however, Moltke warned that Germany would enter the war in circumstances advantageous to her enemies: "Thus the military situation is becoming from day to day more unfavorable for us, and can, if our prospective opponents prepare themselves further, unmolested, lead to fateful consequences for us."[24] On the morning of July 30, Moltke still put little pressure on Bethmann Hollweg for mobilization. He told the Austro-Hungarian liaison officer to the German general staff, Captain Fleischmann, that even a Russian mobilization against Austria-Hungary did not require a German mobilization.[25] Moltke's actions do not suggest a premeditated plot to seize this opportunity to wage a preventive war. His counsel was even moderate and delineated the security concerns that confronted German policy makers.

On the afternoon of July 30, however, Moltke abruptly changed his mind, and he began stridently demanding the immediate commencement of mobilization. Moltke's shift in views played a significant role in bringing on the war. What caused him to change his mind? Historians examining the outbreak of the First World War have long debated this issue. One important consideration was information Moltke received from the foreign ministry and his intelligence services around noon showing that Russian military preparations were no longer limited to Austria-Hungary but included Germany as well.[26] Another, perhaps even more important, consideration seems to have been Moltke's realization that Conrad might stand on the defensive in Galicia and pursue an offensive against Serbia. If this occurred, Germany's eastern frontier would be in grave danger because Moltke depended on a Habsburg offensive to distract the Russians toward Galicia. This fear prompted Moltke to have the Austrian military attaché, Freiherr von Bienerth, send a telegram to Vienna urging Conrad: "Stand firm against Russian mobilization. Austria-Hungary must be preserved, mobilize at once against Russia."[27] These exhortations to Vienna for mobilization conflicted with Bethmann Hollweg's simultaneous efforts to prevent conflict between Austria-Hungary and Russia. When Conrad showed these messages to Berchtold, the astonished Habsburg foreign minister retorted: "Who is in charge in Berlin, Bethmann or Moltke?"[28]

After talking with Fleischmann and receiving later telegrams from Bienerth and Moltke, Conrad replied the following day. Conrad announced his intention to begin mobilization against Russia that very afternoon. Austria-Hungary, however, "will not declare war on Russia nor start the war."[29] Conrad had hoped that this reply would satisfy the divergent German demands of not provoking Russia while simultaneously preparing for war. It would also permit Conrad to continue his deployment against Serbia. "We are not yet clear," Conrad wrote, "whether Russia is only threatening so we must not let ourselves be distracted from our action against Serbia."[30] Conrad's reply only heightened the fears of the German chief of staff. Moltke received this dispatch at approximately the same time Berlin became aware of the Russian proclamation of general mobilization, instead of the partial mobilization against Austria-Hungary. A harried and horrified Moltke quickly telegraphed back: "Does Austria intend to leave Germany in the lurch?" Offended by this rebuke, Conrad immediately responded that Vienna only followed Berlin's lead in not being the first to declare war but to await Russia. Furthermore, because Russia's mobilization might be a bluff, Conrad planned to continue his offensive against Serbia while making defensive preparations in Galicia. Finally, Conrad complained that he had heard nothing of German mobilization: "It will be a completely different situation, if Germany declares that she will prosecute the war with us."[31] The inadequacies of the prewar staff talks are made glaring by these frantic eleventh-hour exchanges between Conrad and Moltke.

By the time Conrad's reply reached Berlin, the German government had already resigned itself to the inevitability of war with Russia. The news of Russian general mobilization forced Bethmann Hollweg to let Moltke and Falkenhayn announce the condition of impending war (*drohende Kriegsgefahr*)—the first step in the mobilization sequence. At 3:30 in the afternoon of July 31, an ultimatum went to Saint Petersburg: "[German] Mobilization must follow, unless Russia ceases any military action against us and Austria within twelve hours and makes a binding declaration to that effect." Bethmann Hollweg was later to rationalize for his fatalistic view about the inevitability of war: "Even if a more rational opinion prevailed in Saint Petersburg, we could not wait passively while Russian mobilization was going full speed ahead so that we would be completely behind militarily in case of war."[32] Bethmann Hollweg's diplomacy of brinkmanship had tragic consequences. The German chancellor pursued divergent aims—preventing a conflict between the great powers, avoiding a diplomatic defeat, and providing for Germany's military security if war occurred—that he could not reconcile.

With war imminent, Moltke wanted a Habsburg offensive in Galicia so he could proceed with the Schlieffen Plan. On the evening of July 31 Wilhelm telegraphed Franz Joseph urging him to mass his armies against Russia:

In this momentous struggle it is of the greatest importance that Austria should direct her main forces against Russia and should not divide her forces by an offensive against Serbia. This is the more important as a large part of my army will be tied by France. In the battle of giants into which we are entering shoulder to shoulder, Serbia plays quite a subsidiary part, which calls only for such defensive measures as are absolutely necessary. A successful issue of the war, and with it the existence of our monarchies, is only to be hoped for if both of us move with our full strength against our new and mighty opponents.[33]

Franz Joseph sent a carefully worded reply August 1. Based on a memorandum prepared by Conrad, the telegram written by foreign ministry officials failed to make clear whether the Serbian offensive would be postponed. Instead, it only promised the deployment of the "great majority" of Habsburg forces to Galicia.[34] If Germany and Austria-Hungary went to war "shoulder to shoulder," they failed to have a meeting of the minds.

The lack of cooperation on strategic objectives and operations plans required a quick remedy. On August 1, the German military attaché in Vienna sent an urgent plea to Berlin:

It is high time that the two general staffs confer with complete candor with regard to mobilization, jump-off time, deployment areas and accurate troop strength. . . . I am once again begging Your Excellency to [take] the necessary steps to provide for cooperation and coherence in the operations against Russia as quickly as possible. Everyone has been counting on the assumption that the two chiefs of staff had developed these close arrangements between themselves.[35]

This plea was but one consequence of attempts by Moltke and Conrad to deceive each other. Moreover, there remained little chance of frankness between the two chiefs of staff because both continued to hope to use the other to gain their own ends. Conrad counted on Moltke's promise of a Narew offensive so that he could go on with his attack on Serbia. Meanwhile, Moltke intended to carry out the Schlieffen Plan, and he relied upon an attack by Conrad's armies to distract Russian forces from pursuing their own offensive against Germany.

That neither chief of staff wanted to coordinate the military operations of his forces reflects an underlying divergence between the political ambitions of Austria-Hungary and Germany. Conrad showed a total disregard of the political and strategic implications of the Schlieffen Plan for Austria-Hungary. He clearly did not understand that the Schlieffen Plan entailed attacking Belgium even before the completion of Germany's deployment. Once put into motion, the Schlieffen Plan meant war, and Austria-Hungary would be caught up in a general European war. Conrad misunderstood the political and strategic importance of the Schlieffen Plan for Austria-Hungary. This misunderstanding, again, highlights the bungling of the prewar collaboration of Conrad and Moltke.

NOTES

1. For the evidence on this, see Norman Stone, "Austria-Hungary," in *Knowing One's Enemies: Intelligence Assessment Before the Two World Wars*, ed. Ernest R. May (Princeton: Princeton University Press, 1984), 57; also see Ratzenhofer MSS, 192, 201.

2. *AMD*, iv, 122.

3. März, *Austrian Banking*, 104.

4. *AMD*, iv, 150–51.

5. Albertini, *Origins*, ii, 664.

6. KA, Befehl des Chef des Generalstabes, Akten "Rückverlegter Aufmarsch," July 13, 1914.

7. See, in particular, the articles published by Stephen van Evera, "The Cult of the Offensive and the Origins of the First World War," Jack Snyder, "Civil-Military Relations and the Cult of the Offensive, 1914 and 1984," and Richard Ned Lebow, "Windows of Opportunity: Do States Jump Through Them?" in *International Security*, 9, 1 (1984).

8. Ratzenhofer MSS, 155–56.

9. *AMD*, iv, 148.

10. Ibid., iv, 162.

11. Winston S. Churchill, *The Unknown War: The Eastern Front* (New York: Charles Scribner's Sons, 1931), 132.

12. Joachim Remak, "1914—The Third Balkan War: Origins Reconsidered," *Journal of Modern History*, 43 (1971): 353–66.

13. Ratzenhofer MSS, 209–10.

14. General Bela von Lengyel, "Die oesterreichisch-ungarische Heeresleitung 1914," *Allgemeine Schweizerische Militärzeitschrift*, August (1964).

15. Straub diary, 31 July 1914, Kriegsarchiv, Vienna. Ratzenhofer supported Straub's assessment of the dangers of trying to rush the *"B"-Staffel* to Galicia, see Ratzenhofer MSS, 207–8.

16. Turner, *Origins of the First World War*, 107.

17. On this strategy to lead a politically united Germany into war, see Jarausch, *Enigmatic Chancellor*, 148–84. Jarausch's account of Bethmann Hollweg's motivations is far more convincing than Fritz Fischer's interpretation in *Germany's Aims*, 50–92. For a trenchant critique of the Fischer interpretation of the war's origins and the July Crisis, see David E. Kaiser, "Germany and the Origins of the First World War," *Journal of Modern History*, 55, 3 (1983): 442–74.

18. See the excellent article by Ulrich Trumpener, "War Premeditated? German Intelligence Operations in July 1914," *Central European History*, 9 (1976): 64–75. In addition, see Dennis E. Showalter, *Tannenberg: Clash of Empires* (Hamden, Conn.: Archon Books, 1991), 69–102. These studies are a useful corrective to the many accounts of the Fischer school on the German military leadership's actions during the July Crisis.

19. Geiss, *Documents*, 282–84.

20. See, for example, Albertini, *Origins*, ii, 488.

21. Fritz Fischer, *War of Illusions: German Policies from 1911 to 1914* (New York: W. W. Norton, 1975), 391.

22. That the Russians began to mobilize considerably earlier than they made out is demonstrated by the prompt arrival in the battle area of units stationed in peacetime in Siberia and the Caucasus. These units could scarcely have reached the frontiers in time for the opening battles if they had been mobilized only at the beginning of August. On this, see Norman Stone, "Moltke-Conrad: Relations Between the Austro-Hungarian and German General Staffs, 1909–1914," *The Historical Journal*, 9, 2 (1966): 216, n. 39.

23. H. von Zwehl, *Erich von Falkenhayn* (Berlin: E. S. Mittler und Sohn, 1926), 57.

24. Geiss, *Documents*, 284.

25. *AMD*, iv, 151–52. Liaison officers were exchanged between the two staffs on July 30.

26. Trumpener, "War Premeditated?" 79–80.

27. *AMD*, iv, 152.

28. Ibid., iv, 153.

29. Ibid., iv, 152.

30. Norman Stone, "Die Mobilmachung der österreichisch-ungarischen Armee 1914," *Militärgeschichtliche Mitteilungen*, 2 (1974): 67–95.

31. *AMD*, iv, 155–56.

32. Jarausch, *Enigmatic Chancellor*, 173–74.

33. *AMD*, iv, 156; this translation is based largely on that which appears in Churchill, *Unknown War*, 122.

34. *AMD*, iv, 159–60; also see Stone, "Moltke-Conrad," 218; and Holger H. Herwig, "Disjointed Allies: Coalition Warfare in Berlin and Vienna, 1914," *The Journal of Military History*, 54, 3 (1990): 265–80.

35. Ludwig Beck, "Besass Deutschland 1914 einen Kriegsplan?" in *Studien*, ed. Hans Speidel, (Stuttgart: K. F. Koehler Verlag, 1955), 102.

Chapter 7

East or West in Germany's Deployment

Despite Moltke's commitment to carrying out the Schlieffen Plan, there appeared a chance on August 1 that Germany might stand on the defensive in the west and concentrate sizeable forces to the east against Russia. Germany, then, would revert to the strategy of the elder Moltke's later deployment plans. At five o'clock on the afternoon of August 1, Wilhelm signed the order for general mobilization, which would begin the next day. On the way to his headquarters, Moltke received an urgent summons to return to the Berliner Schloss, the Kaiser's palace in the center of the city. Once there, Moltke found a meeting in progress that included Wilhelm, Bethmann Hollweg, Falkenhayn, Admiral Alfred von Tirpitz (the navy secretary), and Admiral Georg Alexander von Müller (chief of the Kaiser's naval cabinet), General Moritz von Lyncker (the Kaiser's adjutant-general and chief of the military cabinet), and Gottlieb von Jagow (secretary of state for foreign affairs).[1] The purpose of the meeting was to discuss a dispatch from Prince Karl Max Lichnowsky, the German ambassador in London. This dispatch said that Sir Edward Grey had promised "England would remain neutral and would guarantee France's neutrality" as long as Germany did not attack France.[2] To the group assembled at the Schloss, this was an incredibly good piece of news—Wilhelm even called for champagne to celebrate. This news dissipated the specter of a two-front war and, at the very least, a conflict with Britain. After Bethmann Hollweg, who had worked assiduously to keep Great Britain neutral, explained Lichnowsky's note, Wilhelm turned to Moltke and said: "Now we need only wage war against Russia. So we simply march with the entire army to the east."

Far from being exuberant, Moltke was horrified at the prospect of radically changing Germany's war plan on the spur of the moment. The Schlieffen Plan depended for its success on prompt action by a force of six infantry brigades and heavy artillery, known as the Army of the Meuse. This force, which was kept at combat readiness, was to seize important railroad lines in Luxembourg and capture the Belgian fortress of Liege by a *coup de main*. Moltke told Wilhelm that patrols, followed by the bulk of the 16th infantry division stationed at Trier, were already moving toward Luxembourg. If these forces did not continue their advance, the entire timetable of Germany's deployment would be disrupted: speed was now of the utmost importance because every day lost permitted the Russians to get closer to finishing their deployment, and they had already gained at least a day's advantage over Germany in declaring mobilization. Furthermore, Moltke told Wilhelm that Germany no longer possessed a war plan to manage a deployment against Russia. In 1913, the general staff had discontinued the deployment plan for a war against Russia—the so-called *Grosse Ostaufmarsch*—and there no longer existed an updated version. If Wilhelm insisted on a concentration against Russia, Germany's deployment might fall into irretrievable confusion. "The deployment of an army a million strong," Moltke warned Wilhelm, "was not a thing to be improvised, it was the product of a whole year's hard work and once planned could not be changed. If His Majesty were to insist on directing the whole army to the east, he would not have an army prepared for the attack but a barren heap of armed men disorganized and without supplies."[3]

Angered by this reply, Wilhelm snapped back: "Your uncle would have given me a different answer." Despite the rebuke, Moltke continued to refuse the possibility of changing Germany's deployment plan. The argument grew more heated, as the group pressed Moltke to call back the troops advancing to cross the frontiers of Luxembourg and Belgium. Moltke later recalled: "I stood there quite alone. . . . Of the fact that it was bound to lead to catastrophe for us if we were to march into Russia with a mobilized France at our backs, of this no one seemed to think. Even assuming good will on her part, how could England ever have prevented France from stabbing us in the back?" Finally, Wilhelm cut off the discussion and, ignoring Moltke, turned to his aide-de-camp, Hans von Plessen, ordering him to signal the 16th division not to advance. Moltke complained that he would not accept responsibility for the outcome of the war if the mobilization did not continue according to plan. Bethmann Hollweg shot back: "And I can take no responsibility unless we accept the English offer."

As it turned out, Lichnowsky's message was inaccurate, and this episode has become known as the misunderstanding of August 1.[4] Britain could not restrain France from fighting. Consequently, Wilhelm summoned Moltke back to the Schloss and told him that deployment could go on according to plan.

What this pathetic episode shows is Moltke's childlike faith in one thing—the Schlieffen Plan. His rigidity hampered German decision makers from taking a diplomatic offensive to keep Britain neutral. Instead the Schlieffen Plan was considered Holy Writ—a revelation from the God of

War, with Schlieffen as his prophet. Moltke considered himself a mere technician who refined "The Plan." The suggestion that the Schlieffen Plan be scrapped psychologically devastated Moltke. His argument that insurmountable technical problems prevented any substantial revision of the Schlieffen Plan gives more of an insight into Moltke's limitations as a chief of staff than to the actual capabilities of railroads to move armies.[5]

Both Moltke and Conrad saw the primary value of railroads in the speed with which they permitted deployment. Had not the elder Moltke won the wars of 1866 and 1870 by deploying his armies faster than his opponents? In the spring of 1866, during the mounting diplomatic crisis between Berlin and Vienna, the elder Moltke chafed at the restrictions placed by Bismarck on Prussian military preparations against Austria: "From my point of view, I must express the conviction that success or failure in this war will depend in large part on the decision for war being made earlier here than in Vienna—now if possible."[6] The elder Moltke exploited to the utmost the strategic advantage conferred on him by the rapid completion of deployment. The rapid deployment of Prussia's army enabled the elder Moltke to seize the initiative in the wars against Austria and France. Contrary to the views of those who held that falling behind in deployment did not really matter, the wars of the elder Moltke showed just how important it was in deciding the outcome of a conflict.[7] The advantages bestowed on the side able to deploy more rapidly than its opponents were comparable to those conferred on the side able to "steal" a march on the enemy in an earlier, preindustrial age. Napoleon is attributed with the saying: "I may lose a battle, but I shall never lose a minute."[8] The general staffs of Europe before the First World War took this maxim to heart: military success became equated with speed of mobilization and deployment.

Conrad shared this fear of losing a race in competitive deployments. During the July Crisis, Conrad remained anxious that the deployment of the Serbian or Russian armies would be completed before Habsburg forces reached their concentration areas along the frontiers. Thus, on July 29 Conrad argued with Berchtold that "every day was of far-reaching importance," because "any delay might leave the [Habsburg] forces now assembling in Galicia open to being struck by the full weight of a Russian offensive in the midst of their deployment."[9]

The elder Moltke's success became equated with speed of deployment. This explanation for Moltke's success largely ignored the important role played by incredibly bad generalship in the defeats of Austria in 1866 and France in 1870. Benedek, Bazaine, and MacMahon, whatever their virtues as brave soldiers, were unsuited to lead the great armies entrusted to them; they could not match the elder Moltke in the conduct of operations. It is understandable, however, why military planners drew the lessons that they did from the wars of the elder Moltke. Calculating a railroad timetable in peacetime is easier than coming to grips with the insolvable problem of discerning the intellectual, physical, and moral ingredients that make a great field commander.

These prewar strategic conceptions failed to recognize that strategy is about deploying and using military forces within a political context. By putting emphasis on speed of deployment, the flexibility that railroads also permitted was ignored. During the First World War, railways moved on short notice large bodies of troops from one front to another. The fears of the chiefs of staff in Austria-Hungary, Germany, and Russia that disaster loomed if their mobilization plans were tampered with appear overblown. French railways, for example, transferred seven corps, two reserve divisions, and three cavalry divisions (or the equivalent of two armies) from Lorraine to the Marne River during the last two weeks of August 1914. In October 1914, the Russian General Staff managed to concentrate a force of thirty divisions, under the poor conditions prevailing in Poland, preparatory to their invasion of Germany. During the same period, Conrad transferred the entire Second Army from his right flank in the Carpathian mountains to his left flank in Poland north of Cracow. Finally, when Romania entered the war in September 1916, Germany and Austria-Hungary sent 1,500 trains through Hungary—a number equaling that used to mobilize against Russia in 1914. Within three weeks of Romania's intervention in the war, the Central Powers assembled a force approximately equal to the entire Romanian Army of 600,000 men.[10] These examples show the capabilities of staff planners and railways to move large concentrations of troops within a short period of time.

After the war ended and Moltke's memoir appeared in print telling the story of the August 1 council, General Hermann von Staabs wrote a book showing that a deployment to the east could have been accomplished. Staabs spent most of his military service in the railway section of the general staff.[11] If Germany's leaders told the railway section on August 1, Staabs maintains that it could have concentrated five armies in the east instead of one. Meanwhile, sufficient forces, organized in four armies, would have remained in the west to prevent a breakthrough of the French armies in Lorraine. (See Appendix III for details of Staabs' deployment plan.)

A deployment to the east along the lines suggested by Staabs would not have resulted in a short war. Nonetheless, it would have provided Germany and Austria-Hungary with important diplomatic and strategic advantages. First, a deployment of five German armies in the east need not have entailed the outbreak of a great-power war and undertaking of operations. Moltke's version of the Schlieffen Plan, on the other hand, called for the immediate onset of hostilities. The Schlieffen Plan aimed at nothing less than the decisive defeat of French military power within the span of a single campaign. The success of this scheme depended on a preemptive attack to seize the Belgian fortress of Liege. By abandoning the Schlieffen Plan and deploying about half the German army against Russia, Germany need not have launched a preemptive attack before the completion of deployment. German forces, then, could initially have adopted a defensive stance. Secure on both fronts from a French or Russian breakthrough, Germany would have more time to implement its diplomacy of limiting the conflict to a Balkan war between Austria-Hungary and Serbia.

Secondly, Germany would have provided support for Austria-Hungary's efforts to defeat Serbia. Faced by the deployment of five German armies opposite them, Russian planners would have opted for the defensive war plan known as Plan G.[12] Since Russia's armies under this plan would not pose much of an offensive threat, Austria-Hungary could have gone ahead with Conrad's cherished offensive against Serbia, employing the units of the *"B"-Staffel* in the Balkans. With three armies concentrated in the Balkans, Austria-Hungary would have possessed a two-to-one superiority in numbers over Serbia. This superiority should have enabled Habsburg forces to defeat the Serbian army in battle, occupy Belgrade, and overrun large portions of Serbian territory. The principal purpose behind Vienna's decision for war—namely, the humbling of Serbia as an independent military power—would thus have been achieved. Without the presence of the *"B"-Staffel* in the Balkans, Austria-Hungary lacked the military strength to defeat Serbia, as the campaigns of 1914 were to show.

Thirdly, a successful Habsburg campaign against Serbia would have improved the diplomatic position of Germany and Austria-Hungary in the Balkans. Bulgaria might have seized the opportunity to attack Serbia, to reverse the defeat in the recent Second Balkan War. The 1915 campaign in the Balkans would show that, with the support of Bulgarian forces, a concentric attack against Serbia stood a very good chance of success. With the assistance of Bulgaria, German and Habsburg armies overran the entire Serbian Kingdom in a single campaign. The crushing of Serbian military power and the support of Bulgaria would have also served to discourage Romania from pressing its irredentist claims against the Monarchy. Romania might have even found it far more profitable to take this opportunity to turn against Russia and seize Bessarabia. Further, Serbia's defeat would have no doubt increased Germany's prestige and influence. Likewise, Italy would have thought twice before deserting its alliance partners, securing the Central Powers' southern flank. Thus, the outcome of a successful campaign by Austria-Hungary against Serbia would likely have promoted a bandwagon effect, strengthening the position of Germany and the Habsburg Monarchy in the Balkans, in the Middle East, and in the Central Mediterranean. Russia, on the other hand, would have been in a poor position to change this situation.

Fourthly, if Saint Petersburg decided to push its confrontation to the point of war, Staabs' plan to deploy five German armies in the east would have enabled Austria-Hungary and Germany to inflict heavy defeats on Russia. Germany's armies, together with the three Habsburg armies in

Galicia, would have been in a position to carry out a powerful offensive into Russian Poland. By advancing from Galicia, Silesia, Posen, and East Prussia, German and Habsburg armies could have encircled and annihilated any Russian forces that stood their ground within the Polish salient around Warsaw. Although these losses might not have resulted in a "decisive" overthrow of Russia's military power, they would hurt the prestige of the Tsarist government. Moreover, Germany and Austria-Hungary would have greatly enhanced their security by establishing a defensive glacis inside Russian territory. It is difficult to imagine Russia forcing the armies of Germany and Austria-Hungary off its territory. Russia's strategic problem might have gone from bad to worse if Romania and Turkey jumped on the Central Powers' bandwagon. Faced by loss of territory and military defeats, Saint Petersburg might have had no option but to negotiate an early settlement of the conflict.

What if Russia had refused to cooperate and, in combination with France, had refused to make peace but tried to prolong the contest? In a protracted war the economic weaknesses of Russia and France would weigh heavily against their chances of defeating the Central Powers. By almost every measure of economic power and technological prowess, Germany and Austria-Hungary were considerably superior to Russia and France. The Central Powers, for example, produced more than twice the steel of France and Russia. Paul Kennedy has convincingly argued: "If a lengthy war occurred, in which the industrial productivity and financial-cum-technological capacity of each side became even more important, then the *Franco-Russe* was clearly the weaker, and it is difficult to see how a German-Austrian victory could have been avoided without the intervention of *non*-continental European powers and their economic resources."[13] A further factor often ignored is that Germany and Austria-Hungary also possessed superior naval power, which no doubt would have played a larger role in a prolonged conflict. Thus, even in a protracted war, where Saint Petersburg and Paris refused early negotiations for war termination, Germany and Austria-Hungary could far better withstand the economic strain.

Fifth, campaigns in the Balkans and the east by Austria-Hungary and Germany would have greatly reduced the risk of Britain's intervention in the conflict. By avoiding the violation of Belgian territory and not attacking France, Britain's Liberal government might have failed to agree on the necessity of going to war.[14] Thus, one of Bethmann Hollweg's principal diplomatic goals—namely, the breaking of the Entente—might have been achieved.

Finally, the large concentration of German forces in the east would likely have spared Austria-Hungary the humiliating defeats it suffered during the opening campaigns of the war. In the opening campaign of 1914, Austria-Hungary was left to bear the brunt of Russia's military power, with the result that it suffered serious losses. These defeats greatly weakened the Monarchy by undermining morale, exacerbating preexisting nationality conflicts, and lowering its prestige. On the other hand, victories in these early battles might have gone a long way to restoring the Habsburg Monarchy's standing as a great power. Defeats inflicted on Russia and Serbia would have improved Austria-Hungary's strategic position. Meanwhile, Habsburg battlefield successes might have intimidated Romania and Italy from challenging Austria-Hungary.

Germany's decision to carry out the Schlieffen Plan, in the political circumstances of the July Crisis, was a strategic mistake. It seems that even Moltke later regretted following the Schlieffen Plan. Not long after Moltke was relieved as chief of staff, he told Matthias Erzberger, the leader of the Catholic Center Party, the attack on France had been a mistake. Instead of going ahead with the Schlieffen Plan, Moltke thought that his uncle's strategy would have worked better: "the larger part of our army ought first to have been sent east to smash the Russian steam roller, while limiting operations in the west to beating off the enemy's attack on our frontier."[15] From a diplomatic perspective, the Schlieffen Plan ruined whatever chances Bethmann Hollweg had of keeping Great Britain neutral. It also belied Berlin's contention that war had been forced on her by Russian mobilization: Germany had responded to a Russian provocation by attacking two small neutrals and France. The Schlieffen Plan cannot be considered an "appropriate response" to Russian mobilization: instead of fighting a war to preserve their ally Austria-Hungary, Germany was fighting a war for continental hegemony. To be sure, the Schlieffen Plan came very close to defeating France's field armies. After all, the French called it a miracle that they won the Battle of the Marne.[16] The Schlieffen Plan represented a daring use of Germany's military resources that took advantage of Russia's slower deployment and the relative military weakness of Belgium and Britain.[17] In 1905, during the First Moroccan Crisis when Schlieffen completed the Plan, Russia was prostrate, defeated in the Far East by Japan and wracked by revolution at home. The Russian army posed little military threat to Germany. In addition, the political circumstances surrounding the First Moroccan Crisis bore little resemblance to those that caused the outbreak of the First World War. During the First Moroccan Crisis, Germany faced France in a political test of will. If war had occurred in 1905, the Schlieffen Plan made some strategic sense. In 1914, however, the Schlieffen Plan did not fit Germany's political situation. Bethmann Hollweg's diplomacy of brinkmanship aimed at breaking apart the Entente. Moreover, Berlin supposedly only entered into war to save Austria-Hungary from Russian aggression. Ironically, the foremost proponents of Clausewitz, the German general staff, failed to heed his most important dictum: "No one starts a war—or rather, no one in his senses ought to do so—without first being clear in mind what he intends to achieve by that war and how he intends to conduct it."[18]

If a German concentration promised to bring such important political and strategic rewards, why did Germany's leaders stop updating the *Grosse Ostaufmarsch* in 1913? Considerable controversy surrounds this decision. Some disciples of Fritz Fischer argue that this decision was part of a conspiracy by Germany's leadership to wage a preventive war to gain a Napoleonic hegemony in Europe.[19] This conspiracy theory, however, is seriously flawed. The explanation offered by general staff officers was that the annual revision and updating of a deployment plan consumed a great deal of their time. Their workload grew heavier in 1912 and 1913 when legislation passed by the Reichstag added three new army corps to the German army's order of battle. Already overworked general staff planners were kept busy devising new deployment plans incorporating these new forces. In revising the two major war plans, planners on the German general staff accorded priority to the Schlieffen Plan, and its revision came before an updating of the *Grosse Ostaufmarsch*. They made this decision, in part, because the 1912 war game, involving the deployment of half the German army against Russia, showed that a war on the eastern front defied a quick operational solution and ran the risk of exposing the western front to a French breakthrough. A further consideration was that Germany's military leaders did not think Britain would remain neutral in a continental war. In the wake of the Agadir Crisis of 1911, Britain improved its security cooperation with France and began discussions with Russia. Since Britain was counted as an enemy, there seemed little diplomatic inhibition to an advance through Belgium. Finally, the abandonment of the Schlieffen Plan meant that Germany's leaders had abandoned any hope of a quick victory in case of war with France and Russia. To admit that Germany should not aim at a knockout blow was unpalatable to civilians as well as soldiers. If a quick victory was possible, then, it should be striven after. Even Bethmann Hollweg argued "offense in the East and defense in the West would have implied the admission that we expected at best a draw." The support of the German people might wither if Germany fought for limited aims. Bethmann Hollweg thought: "With such a slogan no army and no nation could be led into a struggle for their existence."[20] Since the chancellor held to these views, it is thus not surprising that the German general staff did not give as high a priority to upgrading the deployment plan against Russia. This explanation, although more prosaic than the one offered by the Fischer school, is nonetheless much more convincing.

NOTES

1. The following account of this meeting is drawn from Moltke, *Erinnerungen*, 19; Correlli Barnett, *The Swordbearers: Supreme Command in the First World War* (Bloomington, Ind.: Indiana University Press, 1975), 3–10; Georg von Müller, *The Kaiser and His Court: The Diaries, Notebooks and Letters of Admiral Georg Alexander von*

Müller, 1914–1918, ed. Walter Görlitz and trans. Mervyn Savill (London: Macdonald, 1961), 11; and Barbara W. Tuchman, *The Guns of August* (New York: Macmillan, 1962), 76–82.

2. Geiss, *Documents*, 343.

3. Barnett, *Swordbearers*, 6–7.

4. See Harry F. Young, "The Misunderstanding of August 1, 1914," *Journal of Modern History*, 48, 4 (1976): 644–65.

5. Norman Stone writes: "The railway-technicians often talked of their great clockwork; but it was a machine that owed something to the cuckoo." See his *The Eastern Front, 1914–1917* (New York: Charles Scribner's Sons, 1975), 78.

6. Dennis E. Showalter, *Railroads and Rifles: Soldiers, Technology, and the Unification of Germany* (Hamden, Conn.: Archon Books, 1975), 57.

7. Once again, see the writings of van Evera, "Cult of the Offensive," Snyder, "Civil-Military Relations," and Lebow, "Windows of Opportunity," in *International Security*.

8. David Chandler, *The Campaigns of Napoleon* (New York: Macmillan, 1966), 149.

9. Albertini, *Origins*, ii, 670.

10. Stone, *Eastern Front*, 265.

11. Hermann von Staabs, *Aufmarsch nach zwei Fronten: Auf Grund der Operationspläne von 1871–1914* (Berlin: E. S. Mittler und Sohn, 1925), 51–62. Staabs' involvement with the railroad section of the general staff ended in 1908. Thereafter he commanded a regiment and served as a department director in the war ministry, before taking command of an infantry division in East Prussia in 1913. Thus, during the six years immediately preceding the war, Staabs had little direct contact with the general staff's operational and railway planning sections. (Information about Staabs' military career supplied to the author by Ulrich Trumpener, the University of Alberta, in a letter dated November 21, 1977.) Despite this period of absence from staff planning, Staabs' improvised deployment plan was not beyond the capacity of Germany's railways, as was amply demonstrated by troop movements undertaken later in the war.

12. On Russian war planning, see William C. Fuller, "The Russian Empire," in *Knowing One's Enemies: Intelligence Assessment Before the Two World Wars*, ed. Ernest R. May (Princeton: Princeton University Press, 1984), 98–126; and Jack Snyder, *The Ideology of the Offensive: Military Decision Making and the Disasters of 1914* (Ithaca, N.Y.: Cornell University Press, 1984), 157–98. Fuller demonstrates that Russian war planners, despite their excellent intelligence clearly indicating Germany's decision to deploy under the Schlieffen Plan the bulk of its forces against France, nonetheless feared that German armies might concentrate in the east and undertake an early offensive designed to disrupt Russia's deployment. If sizeable German forces had amassed in the east, then Russia's armies would no doubt have stood on the defensive, and the forces allocated for use against Austria-Hungary would instead have been deployed to ward off Germany's offensive.

13. Paul Kennedy, "The First World War and the International Power System," *International Security*, 9, 1 (1984): 19. In his recent book, Kennedy argues that Russia's "socioeconomic and technical backwardness" hobbled any attempt to fight a protracted war. Indeed, Kennedy maintains that, despite "all of its own absolute increases in industrial output in this period [before the First World War],

the awful fact was that Russia's productive strength was actually *decreasing* relative to Germany's." See, his *The Rise and Fall of the Great Powers: Economic Change and Military Conflict from 1500 to 2000* (New York: Random House, 1987), 232–42.

14. On the division within the British cabinet over the decision for war, see Wilson, *Policy of the Entente*, 135–47. Lloyd George's decision for war played a major role in preserving the unity of the Liberal party and the government. See the shrewd assessment of the personalities and politics in the decision for war provided by Michael G. Fry, *Lloyd George and Foreign Policy*, vol. 1, *The Education of a Statesman, 1890–1916* (Montreal: McGill-Queen's University Press, 1977), 183–213.

15. Matthias Erzberger, *Erlebnisse im Weltkrieg* (Stuttgart and Berlin: Deutsche Verlags-anstalt, 1920), 80.

16. For a superb assessment of Germany's operational options and chances for victory in the battle of the Marne, see Bradley J. Meyer, "Operational Art and the German Command System in World War I" (Ph.D. diss., Ohio State University, 1988), 85–265. That Germany came so close to success in the Marne battle vitiates some of the conclusions reached by Martin van Creveld about the logistical hurdles in the way of the Schlieffen Plan, see his *Supplying War: Logistics from Wallenstein to Patton* (Cambridge: Cambridge University Press, 1977), 109–41.

17. On the way in which the Schlieffen Plan capitalized on the vulnerabilities of France, Russia, Britain, and Belgium, see the excellent article by Scott D. Sagan, "1914 Revisited: Allies, Offense, and Instability," *International Security*, 11, 1 (1986): 151–75. For a provocative assessment of the role a stronger British army might have played in deterring a German advance through Belgium, see Donald Kagan, "World War I, World War II, World War III," *Commentary*, 84, 3 (1987).

18. Carl von Clausewitz, *On War*, trans. and ed. Michael Howard and Peter Paret (Princeton: Princeton University Press, 1976), 579.

19. See the two articles by the Swiss historian Adolf Gasser, "Der deutsche Hegemonialkrieg von 1914," in *Deutschland in der Weltpolitik des 19. und 20. Jahrhunderts: festschrift für Fritz Fischer*, ed. Imanuel Geiss and Bernd Jürgen Wendt (Düsseldorf: Bertelsmann Universitätsverlag, 1973), 310 ff.; and "Deutschlands Entschluss zum Präventivkrieg 1913–1914," in *Discordia Concors: Festschrift für Edgar Bonjour*, ed. Marc Sieber (Basel: Helbing and Lichtenhahn, 1968), 173 ff.

20. Jarausch, *Enigmatic Chancellor*, 175.

Chapter 8

Britain's Decision for War

The principal strategic drawback for Germany's use of the Schlieffen Plan was that it ensured Britain's entry into the war. Foreign policy issues did not attract much attention from British decision makers during the spring and early summer of 1914. Instead, they faced a mounting domestic political crisis over the provision of home rule for Ireland. This divisive issue even threatened to embroil the country in civil war. Meanwhile, relations with Germany appeared better than any time during the preceding five years. In a celebrated speech, given on July 23, 1914—the same day as Austria-Hungary's ultimatum to Serbia—Britain's chancellor of the exchequer, David Lloyd George, asserted that public opinion around the world would not stand for a continuation of the great-power competition in armaments. He could not "help thinking that civilisation, which is able to deal with disputes amongst individuals and small communities at home, and is able to regulate these by means of sane and well-ordered arbitrament, should be able to extend its operations to the larger sphere of disputes amongst states."[1] That a politician as astute as Lloyd George could be so wrong illustrates the illusions held by many British Liberals on the eve of war. It also helps explain why Britain could not deter Germany from unleashing the Schlieffen Plan.

During the July Crisis, Britain's leaders did not face any immediate security concern for the safety of the British fleet. The fleet had just concluded maneuvers when Vienna sent its ultimatum to Serbia. Britain's Liberal government took several steps to ensure that this naval advantage was not lost. First, Churchill and the First Sea Lord, Admiral Louis Battenberg, maintained the main fleet at its high readiness level. With maneuvers completed, the fleet had been scheduled to draw down its strength as its warships dispersed for training exercises and routine repairs in the dockyards. Second, Grey authorized the Admiralty to issue a public statement to the press about the fleet's readiness for war. Grey thought this announcement might signal Britain's resolve and exercise a sobering effect on Berlin. Third, the British Admiralty ordered the main battleship squadrons to their wartime anchorage at Scapa Flow in the north of Scotland. On the night of July 29–30, Britain's main fleet proceeded without incident through the Straits of Dover on its way to Scapa Flow. Britain, then, was in no danger of its fleet being caught in a surprise attack.[2]

On the other side of the North Sea, the German battle fleet was also mobilized for annual summer maneuvers, which included a cruise to Norwegian waters.[3] Before leaving on his own summer cruise to Norwegian waters on July 7, Wilhelm ordered that the fleet be made ready for action in case a war occurred. Although Wilhelm did not rate the chances of war very high, the navy nonetheless received instructions to begin taking measures to ensure its readiness for combat. The coal supplies at the fleet's major bases were brought up to wartime requirements. Germany's torpedo-boat flotillas were to stay ready. The navy office authorized the rapid completion and manning of the battleships *König* and *Grosser Kurfürst* and the battle cruiser *Derfflinger*, which were under construction in German shipyards. The battle cruiser *Goeben*, then on station in the Mediterranean, also received orders to proceed immediately to the Austrian port of Pola for repairs to its boilers, and workmen from Germany were sent to Pola to hasten their completion. In case of war, the *Goeben* would stand ready to attack French shipping in the Mediterranean. The German cruiser squadron in the East Asian waters commanded by Admiral Maximilian von Spee was instructed to remain in close communication as the crisis unfolded. Finally, the German naval staff questioned the wisdom of proceeding with the fleet's cruise to Norwegian waters. With the British naval forces mobilized and ready for action, the German naval staff thought it dangerous to send the fleet so far from home bases. The German Foreign Office, however, insisted that the cruise go on as scheduled. A cancellation of the cruise, it reasoned, would alert the suspicions of the Entente powers about the coming international showdown. In addition, the German Foreign Office thought that the British fleet would soon disperse. If the German fleet made a sudden movement, however, it might provoke Britain into taking steps in preparation for war. Germany would then face a confrontation with Britain.

As the crisis unfolded, Wilhelm and the German naval staff became more apprehensive about the fleet's exposed position in Norwegian waters. They feared that the British might launch a preemptive attack on the German fleet. The acting chief of the naval staff requested that the German Foreign Office provide early warning of a British attack. Germany's foreign secretary, Jagow, still wanted to avoid a sudden recall of the fleet. On July 23, the day of Austria-Hungary's ultimatum to Belgrade, Wilhelm, aboard the royal yacht *Hohenzollern*, closed in on the German fleet off the Norwegian coast. The chief of the Naval Cabinet, Admiral Georg Alexander von Müller, who accompanied Wilhelm on his northern cruise, recorded in his diary: "the excitement grows. Fleet has established radio contact with us. Today the ultimatum is going to be handed over."[4] Wilhelm ordered the fleet to begin coaling and stand ready to make a quick return to home waters. No longer able to keep up the pretense, Wilhelm directed the fleet to steam back to home waters three days later over the objection of Bethmann Hollweg. Bethmann Hollweg wanted to keep the fleet on maneuvers. A sudden, unscheduled movement of the German fleet, the German chancellor feared, might trigger a British response and escalate the confrontation to include Britain. Wilhelm would no longer have any more of this line of reasoning. He not only feared the danger of a British attack, but the prospect of war with Russia now loomed before him. The German fleet needed to be ready for that eventuality. Accordingly, Wilhelm ordered that the fleet prepare to defend themselves against a surprise attack by Russian torpedo boats. At Wilhelm's insistence, then, the German fleet concentrated in home waters.

On July 31, Germany's Foreign Office warned the German naval staff that war with Britain was inevitable. Jagow, the German foreign secretary, wanted to know whether the German fleet was prepared for the imminent outbreak of hostilities. He also asked whether the German fleet planned to begin the war with a preemptive attack on the British fleet. German staff planners considered launching a surprise attack on the British fleet. This strategy, however, was rejected.[5] The German fleet—to use the parlance of nuclear strategy—could not carry out a successful first-strike. Britain's precautionary mobilization and the deployment of its main fleet robbed Germany of any possibility of successfully making a surprise attack. There was no incentive, then, for German naval planners to launch a preemptive strike during the July Crisis. Instead of striking across the North Sea, the German naval high command was more concerned with avoiding a British attack if war came. Germany's fleet went on the defensive, waiting for an anticipated major British attack that never came. The fleet would remain on the defensive at least until the German army secured its victory over France on land. Thus, the German fleet adopted a defensive stance as it began deploying in the North Sea on July 31 for a war against Britain.

The two navies of Britain and Germany, on which so much public attention and treasure had been lavished before 1914, sat on the sidelines as the crisis unfolded. Each side feared that the other would strike first: the admirals were in the grip of the cult of the defensive. Both sides waited on the defensive, with the strategic consequence that even before the first shot was fired, a stalemate had already set in on the principal naval theater of the war.

With their fleet safe from the danger of surprise attack, British decision makers did not face an immediate threat to their country's security. This safety from direct attack colored the deliberations of Britain's Liberal government in deciding for war. At the end of July, the British government consisted of three main political groupings with regard to foreign affairs. Each of these groupings had powerful adherents. The onset of a diplomatic crisis threatened to provoke a deep intra-party dispute over foreign policy. Prime Minister Herbert Henry Asquith knew his government needed careful handling to prevent a split among its leaders. If a split did occur, Britain might be plunged into domestic political turmoil at the height of the international crisis. It was Asquith's aim to prevent Britain from entering into the war hobbled by deep domestic political divisions. This domestic political requirement played an important part in British decision making during the July Crisis.[6]

First, there existed those in the government who wanted to take a firm stand against any German attempt to overthrow the European balance. Most prominent in this group was Sir Edward Grey and Winston Churchill.[7] Asquith also leaned their way within the cabinet. While willing to enter negotiations with Germany to control the crisis, this group also wanted to make certain that Berlin did not use the opportunity to begin a European-wide war. Thus, Churchill ensured that the fleet was kept mobilized and deployed to its war station. Grey also wanted to reassure French decision makers that Britain would take steps to contest an attack by Germany. This group, however, was decisively outnumbered inside the cabinet. In his memoirs, Churchill wrote: "The Cabinet was overwhelmingly pacific. At least three-quarters of its members were determined not to be drawn into a European quarrel, unless Great Britain was herself attacked, which was unlikely."[8] To be sure, hawks in the cabinet could count on the "unhesitating support" of the opposition Conservatives, whose leadership wanted to take a hard line against Germany. This support no doubt buttressed Asquith's resolve in pushing his government toward intervention to protect France.[9] But Asquith also wanted to avoid being repudiated by the bulk of his own party and then having to form a coalition government with the opposition at a moment of crisis. Consequently, Asquith played for time to rally his party's leadership and rank-and-file behind him. The hard liners, then, could not commit Britain to a war against Germany.

A second group wanted to avoid any entanglement in a European war short of a direct attack on Britain. Led by the Liberal elder statesman Sir John Morley, this group of isolationists could not see how Britain's interests were served by taking a firm stand against Germany. Instead, they feared that a hard line in foreign policy might provoke Germany into action. At all costs, they wanted to avoid triggering a conflict. If a great-power conflict did occur, Britain would best serve its interests by avoiding the conflict. Even the violation of Belgium's neutrality by Germany did not entail nor provide sufficient warrant for Britain's entry into the war.

The third group of Liberal leaders occupied a middle ground between these two extremes. This group made up a majority of the cabinet, and they were decisive in determining Britain's foreign policy stance. Lloyd George and Lord Haldane were prominent in this group, which kept an open mind about Britain's participation in a European war. In Haldane's view, it was unclear whether Britain would be able to stay out of the conflict. His assessment was that Britain needed to steer a middle course between isolation and intervention: "The ideas that on the one hand we can wholly disinterest ourselves [from the war on the continent], and on the other that we ought to rush in are both wrong."[10] While wanting to avoid war, the majority of the government might support the hawks if Germany threatened Britain's security interests. Thus, this group's stance depended largely on Germany's actions.

As the crisis unfolded in late July, Lloyd George and Haldane leaned toward keeping Britain neutral if a war involving the four continental great powers occurred. Lloyd George thought it unlikely that the initial period of fighting in this war would result in one side decisively defeating the other. Since a stalemate was the likeliest scenario, he wanted to preserve Britain's independence of action during the opening round of the conflict. As the other European great powers crippled each other in military action, Britain could build up its forces and ready itself to intervene. Once a battlefield deadlock set in on the continent, Britain could mediate the conflict. This strategy would maximize Britain's bargaining leverage and help ensure that any settlement of the conflict between the two European power blocs secured British interests. For this strategy to work, however, Britain needed to avoid involvement in the initial campaigns and let the belligerents exhaust each other.[11] As Haldane put it, "the real course" that Britain should follow was to be "ready to intervene if at a decisive moment we are called on. . . . [T]his is what we must attempt."[12]

The actions of Austria-Hungary and Germany prevented Britain from adopting this foreign policy stance of waiting and intervening at the decisive moment. Austria-Hungary made almost no effort to enlist British support in their bid to humiliate Serbia. What can be the explanation for this remarkable failure of diplomacy? First, Habsburg decision makers focused their attentions during the July Crisis on the confines of the Balkans. With this narrow perspective, they gave more attention in their strategic calculations to the importance of Romania than to Britain. Second, Habsburg leaders concluded that Britain would likely remain aloof from a continental conflict, even if it included the great powers. A Russian victory, after all, would not serve Britain's interests. Britain, then, according to this line of reasoning, would seek to limit the struggle to the Balkans. This action would tacitly support the Monarchy's planned action against Serbia. Third, the Monarchy's leaders had no intention of letting Britain stand in the way of their attack on Serbia. They understood that their goal of crushing Serbia in a rapid campaign, presenting Europe with a fait accompli, was not likely to find much favor in Britain. Berchtold and Count Mensdorff, the Monarchy's ambassador in Britain, consequently did little to win British sympathies; instead, they aimed at deceiving British leaders for as long as possible about their foreign policy plans.[13]

In their last calculation, the Monarchy's leaders shrewdly estimated Britain's reaction to their design against Serbia. Grey wanted Vienna to open negotiations with Saint Petersburg about the Balkan situation and avoid a great-power confrontation. He also opposed a naked power grab by Austria-Hungary to destroy Serbia's independence and Russia's position in the Balkans. While Grey did not want the Entente to gang up against Austria-Hungary, Britain's foreign policy also aimed at preventing the humiliation of Russia. Grey told Mensdorff: if Austria-Hungary "could make war on Serbia and at the same time satisfy Russia, well and good: I could take a holiday tomorrow. But if not, the consequences would be incalculable."[14] This advice was not what the Monarchy's leaders wanted to hear.

Austria-Hungary's ultimatum caused consternation among British decision makers. Grey characterized it "the most formidable document which has ever been addressed to an independent state." Around Grey, the permanent officials of the British Foreign Office, such as Eyre Crowe and Arthur Nicolson, saw Austria-Hungary's actions as part of a larger showdown between the Triple Alliance and the Triple Entente. Grey still hoped that Germany might play a constructive role in dissuading Austria-Hungary from forcing a confrontation between Europe's opposing alliance blocs. A revived concert of European powers, Grey thought, would avoid escalation of the Balkan showdown.

Berlin, however, refused to play that conciliatory role. Germany's leaders intended to put Britain in the awkward position where it must choose whether to support Russia. Bethmann Hollweg thought that Britain might abandon Russia when facing a confrontation triggered by a Balkan conflict. When Britain proposed a four-power mediation of the Austro-Serb conflict, Germany countered by calling for the other powers to remain aloof and "localize" the clash to the Balkans. Austria-Hungary's actions against Serbia and Germany's unhelpful foreign policy stance pushed Britain toward intervention. The strategic stakes for Britain became much larger. Berlin was making the Balkan conflict a test of Britain's adherence to the entente with Russia. Britain faced a serious foreign policy dilemma that might break the Liberal government and the British commitment to Russia.

Germany's decision to employ the Schlieffen Plan, however, solved this dilemma and forced the hands of British decision makers. When it became clear that Germany intended to invade Belgium and attempt to crush France, a wait-and-see foreign policy might have resulted in the outright defeat of one of Europe's continental power blocs and the dramatic rise of German power. If that had occurred, Britain would have stood little chance of curbing Germany's imperial ambitions. Britain might have had to face a new war where it fought a German superpower without the assistance of any major European allies. In those circumstances, British leaders could not be sanguine about their chances for success. A strategy of mediating the continental conflict did not stand much chance of success if after a short campaign Germany emerged victorious over France. Intervention became necessary to prevent Germany from winning quickly on the continent. Lloyd George, Haldane, and those in the middle of the dispute between British hawks and doves came down decisively in favor of immediate intervention. Only Morley and John Burns resigned from the cabinet.

Britain's Liberal government failed to deter Germany's bid for hegemony. To be sure, even a clear warning of British intervention might not have stopped Berlin from fighting Russia and France. It is entirely plausible that Imperial Germany could not be deterred from provoking a war for hegemony in Europe. The muddled actions of Germany's leaders during the July Crisis nonetheless suggest otherwise. A clear threat of British intervention might have had a powerful deterrent effect in Berlin. Wilhelm and Bethmann Hollweg wanted to avoid war with Britain. At the very least, a stronger foreign policy stance by Britain might have led Germany's leaders to abort the Schlieffen Plan. If Germany had scrapped the hair-trigger Schlieffen Plan, more time would then have existed for joint Anglo-German diplomatic initiatives to work. The "halt in Belgrade" formula, in conjunction with Grey's call for an international conference in London, for example, provided the basis for further negotiations to avoid a great-power conflict. A joint effort by Britain and Germany stood a chance to reach agreement between Austria-Hungary, Russia, and Serbia. Negotiations would only work, however, if Britain made clear its resolve to fight any German bid for hegemony. Cooperation between Britain and Germany required that the British Liberals take a firm stand in advance of hostilities to resist German aggression against Belgium and France.

The politics of Liberal Britain, however, would not permit an early warning of British resolve. Like Bethmann Hollweg, for domestic political reasons Asquith needed to put the blame for starting the conflict onto another country. Asquith had a difficult task in building a consensus for intervention within his cabinet and party.[15] Nothing worked to break this deadlock among British Liberals until the Schlieffen Plan made clear the danger that Britain would face if it stood aside from fighting. From a domestic political point of view, the Schlieffen Plan played into Asquith's hands, making easier the task of uniting his government and party. Preserving unity within his government was no small achievement for Asquith. His party held onto power for almost another year without having to form a coalition with the Conservative opposition. But the cost of settling the dispute within the Liberal government was also high: paralysis in warning off Germany's attack to the west.

NOTES

1. On Lloyd George's stance during the July Crisis, see Bentley B. Gilbert, "Pacifist to Interventionist: David Lloyd George in 1911 and 1914. Was Belgium an Issue?" *The Historical Journal*, 28, 4 (1985): 863–85; and Fry, *Lloyd George and Foreign Policy*, 183–213; John Grigg, *Lloyd George: From Peace to War, 1912–1916* (Berkeley: University of California Press, 1985), 137–56; and M.L. Dockrill, "David Lloyd George and Foreign Policy Before 1914," in *Lloyd George: Twelve Essays*, ed. A.J.P. Taylor (New York: Atheneum, 1971), 25–31.

2. On the decision to mobilize and deploy Britain's main battle fleet, see Winston S. Churchill, *The World Crisis* (New York: Charles Scribner's Sons, 1923), 203–46.

3. See the collection of documents edited by Volker Berghahn and Wilhelm Deist, "Kaiserliche Marine und Kriegsausbruch 1914: Neue Dokumente zur Juli-Krise," *Militärgeschichtliche Mitteilungen*, 1 (1970): 37–58. In addition, see Ivo Nikolai Lambi, *The Navy and German Power Politics, 1862–1914* (Boston: Allen and Unwin, 1984), 416–24.

4. J.C.G. Röhl, "Admiral von Müller and the Approach of War, 1911–1914," *Historical Journal*, 12, 4 (1969): 669.

5. See Grand-Admiral [Alfred] von Tirpitz, *My Memoirs*, vol. 1 (London: Hurst and Blackett, [1919]), 275; A. von Tirpitz, *Politische Dokumente*, vol. 2 (Berlin: Hanseatische Verlagsanstalt, 1926), 5.

6. See Keith Wilson's provocative study *The Policy of the Entente*, 135–47; Fry, *Lloyd George and Foreign Policy*, 183–215; and Steiner, *Britain and the Origins of the First World War*, 215–41.

7. Lloyd George told C. P. Scott of the *Manchester Guardian* that initially "only two members of the Cabinet had been in favour of intervention in the War." Lloyd George was presumably referring to Churchill and Grey. Trevor Wilson, ed., *The Political Diaries of C.P. Scott, 1911–1928* (Ithaca, N.Y.: Cornell University Press, 1970), 96.

8. Churchill, *World Crisis*, 211.

9. See Wilson, *Policy of the Entente*, 135–47.

10. K. M. Wilson, "Understanding the 'Misunderstanding' of 1 August 1914," *The Historical Journal*, 37, 4 (1994): 886.

11. Despite Britain's intervention in the opening campaigns of the war, this strategy continued to guide British decision makers. See David French, *British Strategy and War Aims, 1914–1916* (London: Allen and Unwin, 1986).

12. Wilson, "Understanding the 'Misunderstanding,' " 886.

13. The Habsburg Monarchy's clumsy diplomacy with regard to Britain is ably told by F. R. Bridge, "The British Declaration of War on Austria-Hungary in 1914," *The Slavonic Review*, 401–22.

14. Bridge, "British Declaration of War," 409.

15. On Asquith's wartime leadership, see the sympathetic study by George H. Cassar, *Asquith as War Leader* (London: The Hambledon Press, 1994).

Chapter 9

Conclusion: Why Deterrence Failed in 1914

INTRODUCTION

European security in 1914 rested on deterrence and not on cooperation between the alliance blocs. An alternative framework for European security based on mutual interest and cooperative action to avoid a major war could not be constructed. Great Britain's foreign secretary, Sir Edward Grey, earnestly desired to establish such a framework for cooperation by recreating a concert of Europe, in which the great powers avoided conflict. This vision, however, proved an illusion. The underlying antagonisms of the great powers—the appeals of nationalism, imperialism, and the quest for absolute security—frustrated cooperative action, designed to promote mutual gain. Instead, deterrence provided the basis for international equilibrium. In particular, peace required that the great powers restrain Austria-Hungary and Germany from launching a preemptive strike during a crisis.

Before the July Crisis, Austria-Hungary and Germany had not pushed their confrontations with their neighbors to the point where war occurred. Decision makers in Berlin and Vienna had hesitated to take military action in earlier international confrontations because the stakes did not seem commensurate with the costs of a major war. Both governments took seriously the importance of ensuring that domestic public opinion saw the necessity for a war. In that sense, Austria-Hungary and Germany exhibited self-restraint in their foreign policy. The crises over Morocco and the Balkans consequently passed without war. In 1914, however, self-restraint was missing. What had changed from previous crises? What triggered the breakdown of deterrence in 1914? What actions by the other great powers might have deterred Austria-Hungary and Germany from attacking?

DETERRING AUSTRIA-HUNGARY

A first look at these questions must start in Sarajevo. That Gavrilo Princip's terrorist attack in Sarajevo could set in motion events leading to a general European war illustrates the potential danger of state-sponsored terrorism. State-sponsored terrorism is a form of undeclared war. Serbian nationalist extremists, led by Colonel Dragutin Dimitrijević, plotted to use terrorism as part of a campaign to liberate the Balkan Slavic peoples living within the Habsburg Monarchy. The terrorist campaign planned by Dimitrijević menaced Austria-Hungary's control over Bosnia. Serbian nationalist ambitions posed a serious danger to the territorial integrity and great-power standing of the Habsburg Monarchy. Preventing a confrontation in the Balkans between Austria-Hungary and Serbia required that the government of Prime Minister Pašić curb Dimitrijević's terrorism. Given Dimitrijević's resources and ruthlessness, Pašić had very little room for political maneuver. He faced a grave risk if he tried to prevent Dimitrijević's campaign of terrorism in Bosnia. Dimitrijević was quite capable of carrying out a coup against Pašić's government. Intimidated by Dimitrijević, Pašić became what amounted to a tacit co-conspirator in the terrorism directed against Austria-Hungary. Dimitrijević reduced Pašić to the role of a spectator in the drama unfolding at Sarajevo. The feeble attempt made by the Serbian government to warn Vienna of the plot against Franz Ferdinand shows Pašić's domestic political weakness. Dimitrijević's terrorism made a war between Austria-Hungary and Serbia practically inevitable. Deterrence broke down in 1914 because Austria-Hungary was provoked to take strong action against Serbia.

In a one-on-one conflict, Serbia by itself could not defeat Austria-Hungary. While terrorism might start a cycle of violence and spark a Serb uprising in Bosnia, it could not guarantee success in destroying Habsburg rule. The real danger to Austria-Hungary posed by Serbian state-sponsored terrorism was that a Balkan confrontation might escalate into a larger war involving Russia. The rivalries between the great powers transformed a Balkan contest between Austria-Hungary and Serbia into a great-power conflict. In the struggle between Serbia and Austria-Hungary, the other great powers saw a threat to the balance of power in Europe. Austria-Hungary's deteriorating position within the international system provided Serbia with its opportunity to wrest control of Bosnia from Habsburg rule.

Vienna's clumsy diplomacy helped Serbia obtain outside support. Of particular significance was the way Austria-Hungary's relations with the Entente powers worsened during the decade before 1914. The Bosnian Crisis renewed Austria-Hungary's traditional contest with Russia over the Balkans. Russia's weakened international position in the aftermath of the Russo-Japanese War offered Austria-Hungary an opportunity to improve its position in the Balkans. Austria-Hungary took advantage of this opportunity by formally annexing Bosnia. This move, designed to deflate Serbian ambitions and buttress the prestige of the Habsburg Monarchy, only served to antagonize Russia. Russia's recovery from the war with Japan would prevent Austria-Hungary from gaining the security it wanted in the Balkans. The Russian military buildup increasingly undermined Austria-Hungary's strategic position. By 1916 or 1917, Russia would have outnumbered the forces that Austria-Hungary could amass against it in wartime. In addition, Russia could deploy forces to the frontier faster than Austria-Hungary. The changed military balance in eastern Europe was not lost on the Habsburg Monarchy's decision makers during the Balkan Wars. Russia's leaders attempted to intimidate Vienna into accepting a stronger Serbia by provocative military maneuvers. Saint Petersburg's patronage of Serbia put Austria-Hungary in a strategic vise.

France also saw good strategic reasons to support Serbia. French decision makers came to equate their country's security with sustaining and building up Serbia as a threat to Austria-Hungary. Any gain that Austria-Hungary could make in the Balkans would strengthen the Central Powers against the Franco-Russian alliance. President Raymond Poincaré bluntly told the Russian ambassador that "territorial grabs by Austria affect the general European balance and therefore France's interests." He added that, "if Russia goes to war, France will also, as we know that in this question Germany is behind Austria."[1] Strengthening Serbia would also weaken Austria-Hungary, Germany's main ally. Consequently, France and its allies would then gain in relative strength over the Central Powers. With French financial assistance and arms sales, Serbia modernized its army by acquiring advanced weaponry, such as the 75-mm field-artillery piece. Although Serbia was a poor country, and its army suffered from many material shortages, the Serbs could nonetheless find the modern weapons they needed to mount a formidable defense of their country.

Vienna also managed to weaken its international position by needlessly antagonizing Britain. During much of the nineteenth century, Britain and the Habsburg Monarchy worked together to maintain a balance of power on the continent. Austria-Hungary, however, wrecked the chances for continued cooperation by undertaking a naval buildup in modern battleships during the decade before 1914. This Habsburg force of battleships undermined Britain's naval position in the Mediterranean. The Habsburg naval buildup coincided with Germany's challenge of Britain's naval position. In 1912 Britain tried to manage the naval competition with Germany by sending Lord Haldane to Berlin in an attempt to arrange an Anglo-German arms control agreement. The failure of the Haldane arms control initiative and Austria-Hungary's battleship building forced British decision makers into an unwelcome strategic reassessment about naval deployments. To protect its sea lanes in the Mediterranean, Britain began to rely increasingly on France. Austria-Hungary's naval buildup thus played an important part in pushing Britain to convert the entente with France into a security pact.

By antagonizing Britain with naval shipbuilding, Austria-Hungary hurt its chances during the July Crisis of confining the emerging confrontation to the Balkans. Vienna could not rely on Britain for help in its dispute with Serbia. Moreover, British decision makers did nothing to dampen Russia's rush to deploy military forces and confront Austria-Hungary.

Austria-Hungary faced a further worry in that it could not depend on the support of its allies in a war with Serbia. Nominal allies like Italy and Romania might even jump on the opposing bandwagon and attack the Habsburg Monarchy if it became embroiled in a Balkan war. And in the war, these states did attack Austria-Hungary.[2] This fear that other states would bandwagon with Serbia and Russia against Austria-Hungary played a critical role in shaping the actions of Habsburg decision makers during the July Crisis.

Vienna also faced the frightening prospect that Germany might abandon it. The Balkan Wars of 1912–1913 showed that Berlin and Vienna did not possess a common foreign policy line. Habsburg decision makers could not automatically count on German backing in a confrontation with Serbia, even if the Serbian threat appeared very dangerous to Vienna. The eleventh-hour efforts made by German chancellor Theobald von Bethmann Hollweg to moderate Vienna's demands on Serbia show that Germany was not above trying to pressure Austria-Hungary into softening its foreign policy stance.

In July 1914, Habsburg decision makers contributed to their own problems by provoking a war to destroy Serbia's independence. Despite the provocation offered by Serbia, Vienna made a mistake by responding in such an all-or-nothing way. By adopting the unlimited aim of crushing Serbia's autonomy and partitioning Serbian territory, Habsburg decision makers ensured that the Entente powers would stand against it. Vienna's unlimited aims foreclosed diplomatic solutions short of war. A more limited political aim would have kept the Entente powers from backing Serbia to the point of war. The attack in Sarajevo provided justification for Vienna to take steps against Serbia to preclude further terrorism in Bosnia. No great power condoned terrorism. Austria-Hungary squandered this political capital, however, by demanding too much of Serbia. Instead, the Monarchy's actions threatened to upset the larger European balance of power.

Austria-Hungary's internal political situation helped drive its decision to crush Serbia in 1914. For Habsburg decision makers, the increasing strength of Russia, Serbia, and Italy made more menacing the internal political crisis that gripped the Monarchy before 1914. The Slavic populations of the Monarchy demanded a larger political role. Accommodating the demands of nationalist sentiments through political reform, however, faced serious obstacles. In the eastern half of the Monarchy, the obstruction of the ruling Hungarian aristocracy prevented meaningful power sharing with nationalist minorities. With reform efforts crippled by political deadlock, solving the Monarchy's internal dilemmas increasingly seemed to require the use of force—either a civil war or conflicts against neighboring states. Just as the Monarchy had fought against Italian nationalism in 1859 and Prussia's drive to gain hegemony in Germany, Vienna would not give way to Serbia without a fight.

The Habsburg Monarchy's internal political predicament helps explain Conrad's fixation on the threat posed by Serbia and Italy. The southern frontier of the Monarchy appeared in danger of being rolled back by Serbian and Italian nationalist aspirations. Bereft of its southern Slav and Italian populations, without access to a port on the Adriatic, reduced in territory and population, Austria-Hungary would then cease to count as a great power. Moreover, the leaders of a defeated Austria-Hungary would probably be forced into making concessions to share power with the Slavic nationalities that remained within the Monarchy. After all, the defeat in the war with Prussia in 1866 had paved the way for the extraordinary degree of political clout accorded to the Hungarians. Another major military defeat might then further undermine the internal unity of the Monarchy.

The internal politics of the Habsburg Monarchy shaped much of Conrad's preventive war thinking. Conrad's solution to the nationality problem was to fight a series of preventive wars. In his view, preventive wars would serve a dual purpose. First, a war would crush the military capabilities of Serbia and Italy, rendering them powerless to threaten the Monarchy. In addition, a short, victorious war over a foreign adversary would bolster the regime. Conrad had no precise program for political reform; he simply clung to the crude notion—held by many other statesmen and generals throughout history—that a war would solve his country's internal political problems by rallying popular support for the regime. In the short run, Conrad proved right. The peoples of the Monarchy did enthusiastically rally behind the dynasty in 1914.

Austria-Hungary's internal political problems became a European catastrophe with the assassination of Franz Ferdinand and his wife in Sarajevo. By disrupting the domestic political equilibrium within Austria-Hungary, the murder of Franz Ferdinand transformed a status quo power into an aggressive, revisionist state. The assassination goaded the Habsburg Monarchy to become the first great power to decide for war. Once they made their decision, the Monarchy's leaders moved headlong into the struggle, refusing to recognize any attempts to deflect them from attacking Serbia. Conrad's military plan to invade Serbia, destroy its army in battle, and occupy Serbian territory became the Monarchy's foreign policy. The Monarchy's decision to start a Balkan war set in motion a chain reaction of the great powers attacking each other in the support of allies. The contest between Serbia and Austria-Hungary provided the flash point for a war that would directly involve the European great powers.

In explaining Austria-Hungary's decision for war, nothing is more important than that the victim of the assassination was Franz Ferdinand. Princip's act upset the balance within the Habsburg Monarchy between hawks and doves. Until the assassination in Sarajevo, the Monarchy's leadership opposed the military's calls for preventive war. Franz Ferdinand's assassination, however, removed the most important individual standing in the way of war with Serbia. His assassination appeared an act of state-sponsored terrorism, galvanizing the Monarchy's leaders to strike down Serbia.

Public opinion throughout the Monarchy also rallied in favor of the government's decision for war. The peoples of the Monarchy answered the call to arms with an unprecedented upsurge of loyalty to the dynasty and country. Nationality squabbles sank into the background as the Monarchy's subjects united behind the regime. This consideration played a crucial part in the decision of the Monarchy's leaders to provoke a confrontation. They could hardly envision another opportunity when public opinion within the Monarchy would stand so solidly behind the regime. War temporarily put the Monarchy's nationality problems on hold. Faced by this presumed Serbian provocation, even the Hungarian premier Istvan Tisza could not resist the necessity for military action. Although he did not want Serbian territory, Tisza nonetheless thought that the Monarchy had little choice but to respond militarily to such a blatant act of terrorism. Franz Ferdinand achieved something in death that he found difficult in life: the cooperation of Hungary.

Franz Ferdinand's death also made Conrad's alarmist predictions seem farsighted. Before 1914, Conrad had repeatedly called for preventive war. Yet his power to influence foreign policy decision making remained limited. During the Balkan Wars of 1912–1913, Franz Ferdinand had played the key role in the making of the Habsburg's Monarchy's foreign policy. Conrad's constant calls for preventive war made the chief of staff look ridiculous in the eyes of the heir apparent. The feud with Alois von Aehrenthal had already resulted in Conrad's removal in 1911 as chief of staff. There is every indication that, if the assassination in Sarajevo had not occurred, Franz Ferdinand intended to replace Conrad again. In the aftermath of the Sarajevo assassination, however, Conrad's calls for extreme actions no longer seemed outlandish. Whereas Conrad's earlier calls for war had earned him censure and dismissal from office, his extreme remedy appeared the only solution in 1914. Conrad was on the way out when Franz Ferdinand's assassination gave him at long last a chance to fight a preventive war.

Conrad intended to begin the war with Serbia by deploying almost half of Austria-Hungary's army in the Balkans. This force provided Austria-Hungary with a substantial numerical superiority over the Serbian army. The Habsburg Monarchy could then begin an offensive to break Serbian resistance and establish a more pliable regime in Belgrade. Nothing less than an offensive into Serbia would satisfy the political aims of the Habsburg Monarchy's leaders. The defeat of Serbia would cause a realignment of the Balkan states and enhance Austria-Hungary's security. Bulgaria would jump on the Habsburg bandwagon and work with Vienna in the partitioning of Serbia. Vienna would dictate the establishment of a rump, satellite Serbian kingdom. Romania would end its drift toward Russia and remain firmly in the camp of the Central Powers. Russia would no longer have opportunities to meddle on Austria-Hungary's southern flank. The longstanding rivalry with Tsarist Russia for mastery in the Balkans would finally end with a resounding victory for the house of Habsburg.

Given the high stakes in a major power realignment in the Balkans, Russia could not stand aside and let Austria-Hungary crush Serbia. Russia's leaders saw the Habsburg Monarchy's actions as a naked power grab, forming part of a larger contest with Germany for dominance of Eastern Europe and the Middle East. To back down in the face of pressure from the Central Powers would discredit the Tsarist regime as champion of the Pan-Slavic movement and destroy its domestic political popularity. The regime of Nicholas II had already suffered several major foreign policy setbacks. The fiasco of the Russo-Japanese War revealed the incompetence of the regime and forced an unwilling Tsar to make major political reforms by granting the existence of a parliament. In 1909, Alexander Isvolski's inept foreign policy set in motion another crisis that humiliated Russia. Yet another foreign policy debacle would hurt the Tsar's ability to roll back the concessions he made to prevent a revolutionary takeover after the war with Japan. No major figure in the Tsar's government counseled that Russia should avoid war, even if this led to a conflict with Germany and not just Austria-Hungary. A domestic political imperative spurred Nicholas and his government to fight Austria-Hungary rather than permit a wholesale re-alignment of the Balkan states.

Since Russia supported Serbia, the Habsburg Monarchy could not make a decision for war without first consulting its German ally. In 1914 Germany failed to act as a break on Austria-Hungary's aggressive foreign policy behavior. If Germany had not approved a strike against Serbia, it was unlikely that Vienna would have taken unilateral action. Of course, Austria-Hungary might nonetheless have persisted in attacking Serbia even if Berlin did not give its backing. The stakes, after all, appeared to Habsburg decision makers as nothing less than the survival of the Monarchy. Yet it was highly unlikely that Vienna would follow such a dangerous foreign policy course. Austria-Hungary's leaders were not irrational; they were not beyond deterrence.[3] The combined military power of Russia and Serbia precluded Austria-Hungary from achieving its aim of dominance in the Balkans. Even a hothead like Conrad shrank from fighting outnumbered against both Russia and Serbia. Austria-Hungary counted on Germany deterring Russian intervention while Habsburg forces overran Serbia. And, if German threats to Saint Petersburg did not work, and Russia sub-sequently intervened, Austria-Hungary required Germany to redress the military imbalance favoring Russia and Serbia. Berlin, then, could veto a European war by withholding its support for Austria-Hungary to smash

Serbia. By giving their approval in early July, Germany's leaders removed the last serious obstacle to fighting Serbia. Deterring Austria-Hungary meant getting Germany's leaders to moderate Vienna's actions.

DETERRING GERMANY

Germany's leaders showed little inclination to prevent Austria-Hungary from provoking a confrontation with Serbia. Berlin shared the view that the assassination of Franz Ferdinand required action against Serbia. In addition, German decision makers saw the confrontation in the Balkans as a way to improve dramatically Germany's security position. Germany's leaders, then, encouraged Austria-Hungary to make preparations for an attack against Serbia.

Encouraging Vienna to take a hard line against Serbia did not mean, however, that Germany had identical aims to that of Austria-Hungary. The Habsburg Monarchy's decision for war did not reflect any long-range plan by its leaders to embark on a struggle in tandem with Germany for European hegemony.[4] The prewar staff planning conducted by Conrad and Helmuth von Moltke was not part of a concerted attempt to establish Germany's hegemony on the European continent. Prewar staff planning between Conrad and Moltke does not show a common strategic vision nor political purpose between Germany and Austria-Hungary. Instead, their planning reveals a lack of candor and serious coordination. Both chiefs of staff wanted to entrap their ally to promote their own strategy: neither wanted genuine cooperation with the other. Quite simply, no real coordination in war planning existed between Germany and Austria-Hungary before 1914. Differences in strategic outlook were papered over and obscured by the exchanges between the two chiefs of staff. Consequently, during the July Crisis, Austria-Hungary's military actions showed a remarkable degree of independence from Germany. Vienna's goal was to ensnare its ally. Germany, on the other hand, intended to break the Entente. Later in the crisis, Germany's leaders set out on a war for hegemony in Europe. In striving for hegemony, however, Berlin did not ask for Austria-Hungary's approval.

The July Crisis shows the fragility of the alliance bloc led by Germany. Italy defected from the Triple Alliance, refusing to fight alongside Austria-Hungary and Germany. Since Vienna and Berlin appeared to provoke the conflict, Italy saw no obligation to support its allies militarily. Less than a year later, Italy would switch sides and join the ranks of the Central Powers' enemies. Romania also decided to stay on the sidelines, rather than join Austria-Hungary and Germany against Russia. The lure of acquiring Transylvania proved stronger than that of Bessarabia. Finally, the divergent military strategies of Austria-Hungary and Germany reveal their divergent policy agendas.

By focusing on Germany's responsibility for the war's outbreak, the controversy surrounding the German historian Fritz Fischer's thesis has obscured the roles played by Serbia, Austria-Hungary, and Russia in starting the conflict.[5] The First World War started as a Balkan war.[6] Without the Balkan trigger, Germany's rise in power might never have resulted in a world war. The Balkan beginnings of the war call into question the more extreme claims made by historians of the Fischer school who see the war solely as an outgrowth of Germany's aggressiveness. It is difficult to accept, for example, the view that Germany carefully planned a preventive war from the end of 1912.[7] Germany's decision making in July 1914 shows inadequate coordination among the various departments of the German government.[8] The German government's behavior manifests muddled decision making: Berlin at first provided wholehearted support for Austria-Hungary's action in the Balkans; later it made last-minute attempts to restrain Vienna when Britain became involved in finding a negotiated solution to the confrontation; finally it was thrown into confusion about whether to go ahead with the Schlieffen Plan.

Nonetheless, Germany did not promote international restraint by encouraging Austria-Hungary to undertake a military strike against Serbia. Berlin could have prevented any attack by Austria-Hungary and dampened the prospect for a war between the European great powers. Instead, Bethmann Hollweg, with his diplomacy of brinkmanship, tried to engineer and exploit the emerging crisis. In his view, the crisis was an opportunity to shift the balance of power in Germany's favor. His diplomacy was distinctly provocative and carried a high probability of igniting a great-power war. Once Germany's leaders prompted Vienna to take action, they failed to maintain control of the unfolding confrontation, largely letting Austria-Hungary set the tempo and terms.

This course was dangerous because, given the stakes for Austria-Hungary and Russia, neither intended to back down. It appears that Wilhelm and Bethmann Hollweg initially thought that Russia would back down, just as it had in the 1909 Bosnian Crisis. Within the Russian government, leadership changes made it unlikely that Russia would stand aside and permit Austria-Hungary to overrun Serbia. The changes in Saint Petersburg contributed to a hardening of Russia's foreign policy stance toward Austria-Hungary. V. N. Kokovtsev no longer served as chairman of the Council of Ministers, and Sergei Sazonov did not shrink from the prospect of confronting the Central Powers. During the preceding year, the hawks had gained the ascendancy within Russia's leadership. In these circumstances, Germany faced the prospect of either a war with Russia or dropping its support for Austria-Hungary. If Germany found itself trapped into fighting by its ally, the trap was made in Berlin. Bethmann Hollweg could have avoided this trap and war with the Entente. Although later trying to exonerate himself by saying that he had not wanted the war, Bethmann

Hollweg's foreign policy stance made a war with Russia practically inevitable. His diplomacy took Germany to the verge of war. Once there, he botched whatever chances remained for Germany to escape peacefully from the predicament he had created. Charles Maier is no doubt correct in saying that, while Bethmann Hollweg might not have wanted war, "[t]he problem was that he had not really wanted the alternative sufficiently."[9] As long as Britain's intervention did not appear imminent, Bethmann Hollweg intended to fight. A war with France and Russia was not enough to make him want to urge cooperation on Austria-Hungary in settling the crisis.

The emerging "great game" between imperial Germany and Tsarist Russia for dominion over the Balkans and the Middle East provided the larger setting for the war's outbreak. Austria-Hungary and Serbia formed part of this larger contest. Of course, Berlin did not control Austria-Hungary; meanwhile, Serbia acted independently of its great-power patron Russia. The struggle between German and Russian imperialism, however, does explain why a collision between Austria-Hungary and Serbia was not likely to remain isolated to the Balkans. This struggle intensified in the period before the First World War. As Russia recovered its strength from the defeat suffered in the Russo-Japanese War, Saint Petersburg was less willing to permit German bids to expand its power in the Balkans and the Middle East.

How inevitable was a clash brought on by German and Russian imperialism? Several factors stood in the way of a cooperative diplomatic arrangement between Berlin and Saint Petersburg to arrange a spheres of influence agreement. First, the conflict between Austria-Hungary and Serbia stood in the way of a German-Russian rapprochement. This conflict would require that Germany and Russia exert more control over the parties in the dispute than was likely to occur. Both Austria-Hungary and Serbia would consider a wide-ranging German-Russian agreement as a sellout of their position, and they might work to undermine its conclusion.

Second, Germany's inroads in modernizing the Turkish army and desire to build the famous Berlin-to-Baghdad railroad threatened Russia's southern flank. Germany wanted a strengthened Turkey that was open to German investment. Russia, on the other hand, wanted a weak Turkey and even considered seizing Turkish territory. A settlement of the conflicting imperial ambitions of Germany and Russia in the Middle East would not have proved long-lived.

Third, Russia's military buildup posed the first serious military challenge to Germany on land since the Franco-Prussian War. During Bismarck's tenure as Germany's chancellor, France could not put together a coalition of other great powers to help it overturn the 1871 settlement. Even after the making of the Franco-Russian Dual Alliance, Russia's army lacked the capabilities to mount a sustained offensive into Germany. Despite the alliance, both France and Russia were likely to sit on the defense in case of war. The Russo-Japanese War of 1904–1905 crippled Russian military power. Until the Tsarist regime recovered from the political aftershocks of the revolution that accompanied the defeat in the Far East and rebuilt its armed forces, Russia was unable to contemplate war with Austria-Hungary, let alone Germany. Russia's military recovery, however, threatened Germany's security. By 1916–1917, Russia would be in a position to mobilize and deploy almost as fast as Germany. The increase in Russian military strength and the ability to deploy it quickly became the nightmare of German decision makers. Germany responded by increasing its own army. In their effort to increase their security with regard to Russia, Germany's leaders even dropped their country's naval challenge to Britain. It is difficult to imagine a diplomatic way of dampening these competing military buildups on the eve of the First World War. Arms control had failed to settle the Anglo-German naval rivalry, and there is no reason to suppose that it would help arrest the contest in ground forces involving Austria-Hungary, Germany, Russia, and Serbia.

Fourth, Russia's alliance with France placed it firmly in an anti-German camp. Settling the imperial competition between Germany and Russia also entailed the working out of a new European security framework, which diluted the two rival alliance blocs. While Britain wanted to recreate a concert framework to replace the alliance blocs, great-power cooperation depended on a reduction in their underlying antagonisms. These antagonisms made cooperation between the two blocs unlikely.

In this international setting, deterring Germany meant nothing less than discrediting the plans of the German general staff for a short war in the eyes of Germany's leaders. Carl von Clausewitz, the hard-headed apostle of strategic realism, argued that two considerations motivate decision makers to work for peace: "the first is the improbability of victory; the second is its unacceptable cost."[10] In 1914, Germany's leaders did not think victory was improbable, nor did they think the cost of winning would be unacceptable. The Schlieffen Plan appeared to offer the prospect of winning quickly.

Within two or three years, however, Russia's increased capability to deploy rapidly would close Germany's window of opportunity to amass the bulk of the German army against France and leave only a solitary army in the east along the Russian frontier. The requirement of ever larger forces in the east would eventually have resulted in a reversion to the strategic deployment plans of the elder Moltke. At that point, Germany would not possess the resources to carry out a sweep through Belgium. The general staff's win-hold-win strategy could no longer plausibly provide Germany's leaders with a recipe for victory in a short war. Until that happened, Britain, France, and Belgium needed to do more to convince Germany's leaders of the futility of following a short war, preemptive attack strategy in the west.

Neither Belgium nor France, however, could do much more to deter Germany. As the debate over the three-year law showed, France was already straining its resources to keep abreast of Germany in armaments before the war. Nor would a redeployment of French forces to fight a defensive battle stand much chance of deterring the German general staff from attacking. Moltke's prewar correspondence with Conrad shows that the German general staff carefully considered the strategic implications of a French defensive stance. The German general staff preferred that the French begin the war with an all-out offensive from Lorraine. If the French army attacked, German planners calculated that the campaign in the west might end two weeks sooner than if they stood on the defensive behind their fortifications. Although Moltke thought that the French could prolong the war if they eschewed a major offensive, this scenario did not lead him to consider calling off the Schlieffen Plan. Thus, a heavy concentration of French forces along the Belgian frontier—while it might have offered better protection to northern France—would have made little difference on the German decision to attack in the West. Whether it stood on the defense or not, the French army still represented to Germany's military leaders a tempting target for preemptive attack.

In the case of Belgium, it could have afforded to field a larger, better equipped army and to create defensive barriers against a German attack. A greater Belgian military effort would have forced German staff planners to take more seriously the obstacle of that country's opposition. Yet it is doubtful whether a stronger Belgian army would have deterred Germany from going ahead with the Schlieffen Plan. The open terrain of Belgium made it a natural avenue for a German power drive. As it was, Belgium did not make any heroic exertions before 1914 to protect its neutrality by building up its army and fortifications. Given Belgium's military weakness, Moltke thought that a reinforced army corps would suffice to keep the Belgian army in check. The small, poorly equipped Belgian army and its antiquated fortifications could not hope to stem the massive German offensive.

Deterring Germany from beginning the war with a preemptive strike into western Europe thus depended on Britain's foreign policy and defense stance. Only Britain possessed the power to deter a German offensive in the west. Henry Kissinger is surely correct in contending that the peace of Europe depended on Britain playing the role of balancer.[11] Balancing in this instance entailed that Britain take concrete military steps to deter Germany.[12] Britain's victory in the naval arms race was not enough to intimidate German military planners, even if it deterred Admiral Alfred von Tirpitz from wanting to start a war. Since the mobilization and deployment of the main British battle fleet to its war station did not prove enough of a deterrent in 1914, Britain needed to use other security measures to show its resolve. Instead, Britain needed to take two steps before the July Crisis to enhance deterrence.

The most effective way to deter Germany was to make a defensive alliance with France. A defensive pact, providing a guarantee of France's territory, would have made clear Britain's resolve to prevent Germany from gaining hegemony in Europe. Britain might also have offered a unilateral guarantee of Belgium's neutrality. While these steps might not have impressed German military planners much, they would cause the Kaiser and Germany's civilian leaders to rethink their strategic options. To minimize the provocative nature of this step, British leaders could have made clear that it was strictly a defensive alliance and Britain would not join France in an attack on Germany. Thus, Britain would be offering a guarantee of the existing frontiers of western Europe—a Locarno Pact to dampen aggressive action by either France or Germany.

Britain needed to go beyond diplomatic measures, however, to promote deterrence. To ensure that Britain's credibility was not called into question, an increase in the strength and readiness of its army for fighting in western Europe was necessary. One way to accomplish this was by introducing conscription. Conscription could have been used to increase the combat readiness of the Territorial Army—Britain's second-line units—dramatically augmenting the size of its army. F. E. Smith, one of the leading lights of the Britain's prewar Conservative Party, forcefully advocated conscription. He argued that a British military buildup would preserve the peace of Europe. Smith declared: "There would be no war in Europe—and I go further; I say there would be no apprehension of war in Europe—today, if a million English citizens had been trained in those arts of self-defense which have never been forgotten by any great country except in the period of its decay and as an incident in its dissolution."[13] Smith's assessment that Britain was in decay on the eve of the First World War can be debated. The introduction of conscription would have shown Britain's readiness to take on an obligation to prevent any German takeover of Belgium, France, or the Netherlands.

The problem with this policy prescription to promote deterrence is that Britain's Liberal government had no intention of resorting to peacetime conscription. Even after the start of fighting, the Liberals did not institute conscription, relying initially instead on the flood of volunteers to enlarge the British army. The introduction of conscription, then, was outside the realm of practical politics.

Conscription was not really necessary, however. Britain possessed a substantial army in 1914. By the end of 1914, 13 front-line divisions were available for service in France. At least another 18 divisions, made up of the Territorial Army, troops culled from the navy, and contingents from Canada, Australia, and New Zealand, were undergoing training that would enable them to go into battle in 1915. These forces, committed to prompt action in France, were sufficient to ensure that Germany could not win quickly in the initial rounds of fighting. What was lacking in 1914 was not the requisite ground forces, but the political will to stand up to Germany.

None of the measures that might have deterred Germany, although widely discussed in British policy making circles before 1914, stood much chance of getting implemented by Britain's Liberal government. Perhaps a Conservative government, with a commanding lead in the House of Commons, might have adopted a more overt anti-German foreign policy. Yet it is uncertain that even a Conservative government would undertake measures certain to prove unpopular with a large segment of British public opinion. Nonetheless, Britain needed to construct an anti-German front in western Europe. Instead, Britain wavered between appeasement and deterrence. The most serious strategic failure committed by Britain's last Liberal government was that it needed to do more diplomatically to deter Germany from attacking in the west.

Sir Edward Grey understood that Britain's foreign policy must try to strengthen politically those decision makers within the German government who wanted to avoid war. According to this view, Germany's leaders were divided into the standard hawks and doves. Britain needed to help the doves keep control of Germany's foreign policy. Grey quite correctly identified Bethmann Hollweg as someone who wanted to avoid a war between Britain and Germany. The outbreak of war showed that this attempt to promote cooperative action with the German government failed. On August 4, 1914, the day Britain declared war, Grey told the American ambassador: "we must remember that there are two Germanys. There is the Germany of men like ourselves. . . . Then there is the Germany of men of the war party. The war party got the upper hand."[14] To prevent the "war party" from gaining control, Britain had to do more to educate Bethmann Hollweg of the risks associated with the strategy developed by the German general staff. That the German chancellor might try to redirect German strategy in an attempt to avoid war with Britain cannot be dismissed out of hand. Bethmann Hollweg had already tried to improve Anglo-German relations by attempting to prevent Tirpitz from obtaining further increases for the German navy. But he would have to do more to control Germany's decision making, including an effort to criticize the strategic tenets of the Schlieffen Plan. This would have embroiled Bethmann Hollweg in a serious civil-military dispute. The problem with Grey's analysis of German decision making is that appeasement would not strengthen Bethmann Hollweg's position within the German government. Bethmann Hollweg was no dove. In response to Russia's military buildup, he supported increases in the German army. Further, during the July Crisis, he sided with the war party by countenancing a European-wide war. Given Bethmann Hollweg's views, perhaps the best that Britain could have done was to deter Germany from attacking France during the initial stage of fighting.

Bethmann Hollweg saw the circumstances in the summer of 1914 as propitious for fighting. Austria-Hungary's participation was ensured. In previous crises over Morocco, for instance, Germany could not count unconditionally on Austria-Hungary taking part in a conflict with France and Russia. Because the July Crisis originated in a confrontation embroiling Austria-Hungary with Serbia and Russia, Berlin did not have to fear abandonment by its ally. Germany's alliance with Austria-Hungary, then, did not act as a break on an aggressive foreign policy line.

In addition, Bethmann Hollweg shrewdly judged that he could make Russia look like the aggressor, and this would ease his task of guaranteeing that German public opinion would rally behind the government. Bethmann Hollweg took great pains to make it appear that Russia was preparing to strike the first blow. This effort paid enormous political dividends in ensuring social peace. No peace party that stood against the entry into war existed in Germany. Quite the contrary, even the anti-government Social Democrats applauded a war against Russia. War was made to appear the last resort, even if it was not. Moreover, the losses of the initial battles and the failure to win quickly over France did not break the popular resolve to fight imparted by Bethmann Hollweg's management of German public opinion. Thus, given Bethmann Hollweg's skillful handling of German public opinion, there was no domestic political impediment to war.

To induce Berlin into a more cooperative foreign policy stance during the July Crisis, Britain needed to adopt a harder diplomatic line. During the Agadir Crisis three years before, David Lloyd George's Mansion House speech warned Germany's leaders against provoking a war with France. Britain needed to send a similar warning during the last week of July. To prevent Germany's leaders from resorting to a preemptive attack strategy, Britain needed to make clear to them the potential pitfalls of their actions, showing that they could not plausibly expect to defeat France and obtain hegemony. At the very least, Britain should have warned Germany of the consequences it would face by trying to bring about the collapse of French power. Britain might have deterred Germany from using the Schlieffen Plan. The domestic politics of Liberal England, however, precluded the dispatch of a clear deterrent warning. During the July Crisis, Britain initially wanted to back away from playing the role of balancer. Consequently, Germany's leaders discounted the strategic implications of British intervention as they embarked on a desperate gamble to achieve hegemony in Europe. Only when Germany's behavior proved provocative did Britain's foreign policy stance change. The July Crisis thus provides yet another example of where the domestic politics of a liberal democracy inhibited it from balancing in a timely way, failing to deter an aggressive challenger from upsetting the international status quo.[15]

Germany's attack into western Europe posed a danger to the balance of power on the continent and triggered Britain's intervention. Britain's lead-

ers understood German hegemony on the continent would greatly undermine their country's security. After overrunning France, Germany could
consider devoting considerable resources to building up its navy and
ending Britain's naval mastery. Bethmann Hollweg considered such a
course in the fall of 1914, when it appeared that Germany stood on the verge
of defeating France. Reparations extracted from France could be used to
finance a larger German naval buildup. German hegemony in Europe
might lead to an end of Britain's naval mastery.

Having failed to deter Germany from aggressive action, Britain's leaders found the cost of rolling back German territorial gains hideously
expensive. British forces suffered over 700,000 fatalities in the effort to
defeat the German army on the Western Front in France. This was the price,
however, required to defeat Germany's imperial ambitions. Germany
intended to achieve undisputed leadership of Europe by imposing puni-
tive peace settlements on its enemies and reducing its ally Austria-Hungary to the status of a satellite kingdom. Defeating Germany's bid for
hegemony would prove even more costly for Britain than did the fight to
overthrow Napoleon's empire a century before. Deterring German aggression in 1914 would have been far less costly than having to defeat Germany
in war.

Germany's leaders were not strategically autistic. The actions of other
states could alter Germany's strategic behavior. The so-called misunderstanding of August 1 shows that Britain possessed the power to get Germany's leaders to do something they would otherwise not consider
doing—drop the Schlieffen Plan. Upon receiving what they thought was a
British offer of neutrality, Wilhelm and Bethmann Hollweg moved to
change Germany's strategy. This step horrified Moltke and provoked a
civil-military confrontation among Germany's leaders over strategy. Wilhelm and Bethmann Hollweg, however, could and did overrule the chief of
staff, brushing aside Moltke's threat to resign. Of course, Britain did not
make such an offer. When Germany's leaders realized their error, Moltke
received permission to go ahead with the Schlieffen Plan.

This episode provides an opportunity to assess the importance of prewar
military staff planning in driving the great powers to war in 1914. To many
historians and political scientists who have examined the outbreak of the
First World War, these plans constituted a doomsday procedure, prepro-
grammed military offensives that foreclosed diplomatic options to prevent
fighting.[16] According to this view, political leaders panicked under conditions of crisis, losing control over foreign policy and strategy decision
making. Yet Germany's political leaders did not lose control. Wilhelm and
Bethmann Hollweg could control Moltke if they wanted to. They might
have moderated Germany's foreign policy course, worked to limit Vienna's
designs in the Balkans, while carrying out a defensive deployment scheme
against Russia and France. Faced by a heavy concentration of German

forces along its borders, Russia could not have successfully attacked Austria-Hungary. A defensive deployment by Germany, then, would have given Berlin more time to work with Britain to arrange a political settlement of the confrontation in Eastern Europe. Instead, Germany's leaders opted to carry out the Schlieffen Plan. Germany's use of the Schlieffen Plan ensured that the July Crisis would not end with a negotiated settlement. There is much to recommend to A.J.P. Taylor's contention: "When cut down to essentials, the sole cause for the outbreak of war in 1914 was the Schlieffen Plan."[17] While the Schlieffen Plan was a "pre-programmed" strategic package, Germany's leaders could change the program.

Germany, then, must bear responsibility for converting a Balkan standoff into a European-wide war by using the Schlieffen Plan. By starting the war with the Plan, Germany's leaders were attempting to overthrow the balance of power. It was not just an operational plan: it was a declaration of Germany's aims on the European continent. Germany's army intended to inflict a crushing defeat on French military power. With the collapse of French resistance, Germany's leaders could dictate the peace. By redrawing Europe's frontiers, Germany would garner more territory, access to resources, and security from invasion.

In taking this first step into war, German decision makers ran great risks in return for high rewards. Germany's military leaders wanted to hit hard and first. Although a preemptive strike might have made operational sense, the Schlieffen Plan was a political and strategic mistake. Bethmann Hollweg understood that completely defeating France would overthrow the European balance of power and bring about Britain's intervention. In 1912, he wrote to a friend: "Britain continues to uphold the policy of the balance of power and that it will therefore stand up for France if in a war the latter runs the risk of being destroyed by us." Yet, while Bethmann Hollweg understood the problem of obtaining Britain's neutrality, he did not go nearly far enough in trying to address the problem. Bethmann Hollweg's attempt to secure British neutrality by making a pledge not to take territory from France in the wake of a French military defeat was pitiful.[18] He did not face squarely the trade-off that Britain's neutrality required a reorientation of Germany's strategy. By using the Schlieffen Plan, Germany's leaders provoked Britain's entry into the war. In doing this, they contrived to forge the coalition that eventually defeated their attempt to make Germany into a superpower.

NOTES

1. D.C.B. Lieven, *Russia and the Origins of the First World War* (New York: St. Martin's Press, 1983), 48.

2. On weak states and the bandwagoning phenomenon, see Randall L. Schweller, "Bandwagoning for Profit: Bringing the Revisionist State Back In," *International Security*, 19, 1 (1994): 72–107.

3. Colin Gray has suggested that "Austria-Hungary, Hitler's Germany, and the Japanese Empire all, on their own reasoning, had to go to war. They were beyond deterrence." Colin S. Gray, *Strategic Studies: A Critical Assessment* (Westport, Conn.: Greenwood Press, 1982), 87–88.

4. Conrad did not want Austria-Hungary to be reduced to the status of Germany's satellite. He considered the Habsburg Monarchy an independent great power, with foreign policy aims that did not necessarily coincide with Germany's goals. During the war, Conrad constantly sought to prevent the military subordination of Habsburg forces to German command, and he often expressed divergent views on foreign policy and strategy. During the war, he even considered Germany as Austria-Hungary's "secret enemy." See Gary W. Shanafelt, *The Secret Enemy: Austria-Hungary and the German Alliance, 1914–1918* (New York: Columbia University Press, 1985).

5. A notable exception is Paul Schroeder, "World War I as Galloping Gertie: A Reply to Joachim Remak," *The Journal of Modern History*, 44 (1972): 319–45.

6. See Joachim Remak, "1914—The Third Balkan War: Origins Reconsidered," *The Journal of Modern History*, 43 (1971): 353–66.

7. See the articles by Fischer's disciple Adolf Gasser, "Deutschlands Entschluss zum Präventivkrieg 1913–1914," in *Discordia Concors: Festschrift für Edgar Bonjour*, ed. Marc Sieber (Basel: Helbing und Lichtenhahn, 1968); Adolf Gasser, "Der deutsche Hegemonialkrieg von 1914," in *Deutschland in der Weltpolitik des 19. und 20. Jahrhunderts: Festschrift für Fritz Fischer*, ed. Imanuel Geiss and Bernd Jürgen Wendt (Düsseldorf: Bertelsmann Universitätsverlag, 1973); and John C.G. Röhl, *The Kaiser and his Court: Wilhelm II and the Government of Germany* (Cambridge: Cambridge University Press, 1994), 162–89.

8. Perhaps the most judicious critique of the Fischer interpretation was one of the earliest, see Klaus Epstein, "German War Aims in the First World War," *World Politics*, 15, 1 (1962): 163–85.

9. Charles S. Maier, "Wargames: 1914–1919," *The Journal of Interdisciplinary History*, 18, 4 (1988): 849.

10. Carl von Clausewitz, *On War* (Princeton: Princeton University Press, 1976), 91.

11. Henry Kissinger, *Diplomacy* (New York: Simon and Schuster, 1994), 176.

12. See Donald Kagan's very perceptive analysis in "World War I, World War II, World War III," *Commentary*, 84, 3 (1987).

13. John Campbell, *F.E. Smith: First Earl of Birkenhead* (London: Pimlico edition, 1991), 369.

14. Quoted in David Reynolds, *Britannia Overruled: British World Policy and World Power in the Twentieth Century* (London: Longman, 1991), 101.

15. On this issue, see Robert G. Kaufman, "'To Balance or To Bandwagon?' Alignment Decisions in 1930s Europe," *Security Studies*, 1, 3 (1992): 417–47.

16. Henry Kissinger sees mobilization in 1914 as a "doomsday procedure [that] effectively removed the *casus belli* from political control." *Diplomacy*, 202.

17. A.J.P. Taylor, *War by Timetable: How the First World War Began* (London: Macdonald, 1969), 121.

18. Fritz Fischer, "The Miscalculation of English Neutrality: An Aspect of German Foreign Policy on the Eve of World War I," in *The Mirror of History: Essays in Honor of Fritz Fellner*, ed. Solomon Wank (Santa Barbara, Calif.: ABC-Clio, 1988), 374.

Appendix I

Austria-Hungary's Mobilization Calendar

Date	*"B"*		*"R"*		Remarks
	"Alarm"	*Mob.*	*"Alarm"*	*Mob.*	
		Day			Remarks
July 25	–	–	–	–	9:30 p.m., "B" mob order
26	–	–	–	–	Sunday
27	1	–	–	–	"B"-alarm transports begin deployment at 12:00 noon
28	2	1	–	–	M-day for "B"
29	3	2	–	–	
30	4	3	–	–	"B" transports begin deployment at 12:01 a.m.
31	–	4	–	–	
Aug. 1	–	5	–	–	
2	–	6	1	–	"R"-alarm transports begin deployment at 12:00 noon
3	–	7	2	–	
4	–	8	3	1	M-day for "R"
5	–	9	4	2	
6	–	10	5	3	"R" transports begin deployment at 12:01 a.m.
7	–	11	6	4	

Source: Rudolf Kiszling, "The Mobilization of the Great Powers in the Summer of 1914: Austria-Hungary," trans. F. W. Merten *Berliner Monatschefte* (1936).

Appendix II

Tabular Overview of the Movements of the *"B"-Staffel* in 1914

Military Formations:	Their Movements
IV Corps (3 infantry divisions)	One infantry division remained on the Serbian Front. Two divisions sent to Galicia, where they arrived on September 7.
VII Corps (3 infantry divisions)	After being initially deployed to the Balkans, the entire corps went to Galicia, where it arrived on August 27.
VIII Corps (3 infantry divisions)	Two divisions and the corps headquarters remained on the Serbian front, while the third division went directly to Galicia with the *"A"-Staffel*.
IX Corps (2 infantry divisions)	After initially deploying to the Balkans, one division remained behind on the Serbian front, while another moved to Galicia, where it arrived on August 27.
10th Cavalry Division	Sent to Galicia on August 24.
Army High Command Reserves (1 infantry division, 1 cavalry division)	These forces went directly to Galicia.

Source: Norman Stone, "Die Mobilmachung der Österreichisch-ungarischen Armee 1914," *Militärgeschichtliche Mitteilungen* (1974), 94.

Appendix III

Staabs' Deployment East

EASTERN ARMIES

First Army:
The Guard, I, II, and Guard Reserve infantry corps, and the Guard and 2nd cavalry divisions would be deployed in East Prussia on the front Tilsit to Gumbinnen.

Eighth Army:
The X, XVII, I Reserve, and X Reserve infantry corps, the 3rd Reserve division, and the 1st cavalry division would be deployed on a line from Gumbinnen to Marggravowa.

Second Army:
The III, IV, XX, III Reserve, and IV Reserve infantry corps would be deployed on the front between Lyck to Rudzany.

Third Army:
The XII, XIX, V Reserve, and XII Reserve infantry corps deployed on a line from Ortelsburg through Soldau to Thorn.

Fourth Army:
The V, VI, and VI Reserve infantry corps, and the 5th and 8th cavalry divisions would be deployed in Silesia on a front from Ostrowo to Kreuzburg.

WESTERN ARMIES

Seventh Army:
The VII infantry corps and the 9th cavalry division would provide border security for the city of Cologne along the Belgian frontier. The IX and XI infantry corps would be positioned west of Cologne, with the VII Reserve, IX Reserve, and XVIII Reserve corps deployed in the cities of the upper Rhine.

Fifth Army:
The VIII, XIII, XVI, XVIII, and VIII Reserve infantry corps and the 3rd and 6th cavalry divisions would be deployed around the fortress of Metz and along the Saar River.

Sixth Army:
The XXI, I Bavarian, II Bavarian, and III Bavarian infantry corps, and the 7th cavalry division would be deployed in Lorraine.

Army Detachment: The XIV and XV infantry corps would be deployed in Alsace covering the city of Strassburg.

Front Reserve: The XIV Reserve and I Bavarian Reserve infantry corps would be used as a general reserve for all the armies on the Western Front.

Source: Hermann von Staabs, *Aufmarsch nach zwei Fronten: Auf Grund der Operationspläne von 1871-1914* (Berlin: E.S. Mittler und Sohn, 1925), pp. 57-60.

Bibliography

ARCHIVAL SOURCES

Kriegsarchiv, Vienna:

Files of the Military Chancellory of the Archduke Franz Ferdinand
Files of the Operations Bureau, General Staff
Ratzenhofer Collection
Straub diary

Hoover Institution Archives:

Golovine Manuscript Collection
Ratzenhofer Manuscript Collection

U.S. Army Military History Research Collection, U.S. Army War College Archives, Carlisle Barracks, Pennsylvania

de Bartha. "The Austro-Hungarian General Staff." Translated by J. B. Robinson. August 1946.
Kiszling, Rudolf. "The Mobilization of the Great Powers in the Summer of 1914: Austria-Hungary." Translated by F. W. Merten. *Berliner Monatschefte* (March 1936).
von Pitreich, Max. "The Initial Austro-Hungarian Operations Against Russia in the World War and the Siedlce Problem."

PUBLISHED DOCUMENTS, MEMOIRS, DIARIES

von Bardolff, K. *Soldat im Alten Oesterreich*. Jena: E. Diderichs, 1938.

Berghahn, Volker and Wilhelm Deist. "Kaiserliche Marine und Kriegsausbruch 1914: Neue Dolumente zur Juli-Krise." *Militärgeschichtliche Mitteilungen*, 1 (1970).

British Documents on the Origins of the War, 1898–1914. 11 vol. Edited by G. P. Gooch and Harold Temperley. London: His Majesty's Stationery Office, 1926–1938.

Conrad von Hötzendorf, Franz. *Aus meiner Dienstzeit, 1906–1918*. 5 vols. Vienna: Rikola Verlag, 1921–1925.

———. *Die Gefectsausbildung der Infanterie*. 4th ed. Vienna: Verlag von L.W. Seidel und Sohn, 1907.

———. *Private Aufzeichnungen*, edited by Kurt Peball. Vienna: Amalthea Verlag, 1977.

Conrad von Hötzendorf, Gina. *Mein Leben mit Conrad von Hötzendorf*. Graz: Verlag Styria, 1963.

Cramon, August. *Unser österreich-ungarischer Bundesgenosse im Weltkriege*. Berlin: E. S. Mittler, 1920.

Die Deutschen Dokumente zum Kriegsausbruch. 3 vols. Karl Kautsky collection, edited by Walter Schücking and Max Montgelas. Berlin: Deutsche Verlagsgesellschaft für Politik und Geschichte, 1919.

Erzberger, Matthias. *Erlebnisse im Weltkrieg*. Stuttgart and Berlin: Deutsche Verlags-anstalt, 1920.

Geiss, Imanuel, ed. *July 1914: The Outbreak of the First World War, Selected Documents*. New York: W. W. Norton, 1967.

von Kuhl, Hermann. *Der Weltkrieg, 1914–1918*. 2 vols. Berlin: Verlag Tradition Wilhelm Rolf, 1929.

von Moltke, Graf [Helmuth]. *Die deutschen Aufmarschpläne, 1871–1890*, edited by D. von Schmerfeld. Berlin: E. S. Mittler und Sohn, 1929.

von Moltke, Helmuth. *Erinnerungen, Briefe, Dokumente, 1877–1916*. Stuttgart: Der Kommende Tag A. G., 1922.

von Müller, Georg. *The Kaiser and His Court: The Diaries, Notebooks and Letters of Admiral Georg Alexander von Müller, 1914–1918*, edited by Walter Görlitz, and translated by Mervyn Savill. London: Macdonald, 1961.

Österreich-Ungarns Aussenpolitik von der bosnischen Krise 1908 bis zum Kriegsausbruch 1914. 9 vols. Edited by Ludwig Bittner and Hans Uebersberger. Vienna: Österreichischer Bundesverlag für Unterricht, Wissenschaft, und Kunst, 1930.

Österreich-Ungarns letzter Krieg, 1914–1918. Vols. 1 and 5. Herausgegeben vom Österreichischen Bundesministerium für Heereswesen und vom Kriegsarchiv. Vienna: Verlag Militärwissenschaftlichen Mitteilungen, 1929.

Sazonov, Serge. *Fateful Years, 1909–1916*. London: Jonathan Cape, 1928.

Stokes, Gale. "The Serbian Documents from 1914: A Preview." *Journal of Modern History*, 48, 3 (September 1976): on-demand supplement.

Stürgkh, Count Josef. *Im Deutschem Hauptquartier*. Leipzig: Paul List Verlag, 1921.

von Tirpitz, Grand-Admiral [Alfred]. *My Memoirs*. Vol. 1. London: Hurst and Blackett, [1919].

———. *Politische Dockumente*. Vol. 2. Berlin: Hanseatische Verlagsanstalt, 1926.

Der Weltkrieg 1914 bis 1914. Vols 1 and 2. Bearbeitet im Reichsarchiv. Berlin: E. S. Mittler und Sohn, 1925.

Wilson, Trevor, editor. The Political Diaries of C. P. Scott, 1911–1928. Ithaca, N.Y.: Cornell University Press, 1970.

Windischgrätz, Prince Ludwig. *My Memoirs*. Boston: Houghton Mifflin, 1921.

BOOKS AND DISSERTATIONS

Albertini, Luigi. *The Origins of the War of 1914*. 3 vols. London: Oxford University Press, 1953.

Angell, Norman. *The Great Illusion: A Study of the Relation of Military Power in Nations to their Economic and Social Advantage*. New York: G. P. Putnam's Sons, 1911.

Aron, Raymond. *Clausewitz: Philosopher of War*, translated by Christine Booker and Norman Stone. London: Routledge and Kegan Paul, 1983.

Asprey, Robert B. *The Panther's Feast*. London: Jonathan Cape, 1959.

der Bagdasarian, Nicholas. *The Austro-German Rapprochement, 1870–1879: From the Battle of Sedan to the Dual Alliance*. Rutherford, N.J.: Fairleigh Dickinson University Press, 1976.

Barnett, Corelli. *The Swordbearers: Supreme Command in the First World War*. Bloomington, Ind.: Indiana University Press, 1963.

Beck, Ludwig. *Studien*, edited by Hans Speidel. Stuttgart: K. F. Koehler Verlag, 1955.

Bloch, I. S. *The Future of War in Its Technical, Economic and Political Relations: Is War Now Impossible?* New York: Doubleday and McClure, 1899.

Bracken, Paul. *The Command and Control of Nuclear Weapons*. New Haven, Conn.: Yale University Press, 1983.

Brodie, Bernard. *Strategy in the Missile Age*. Princeton: Princeton University Press, 1971.

Bucholz, Arden. *Moltke, Schlieffen, and Prussian War Planning*. New York: Berg, 1991.

Bundesministerium für Landesverteidigung. *Unser Heer*. Vienna: Fürlinger, 1963.

Campbell, John. *F. E. Smith: First Earl of Birkenhead*. London: Pimlico, 1991

Cassar, George H. *Asquith as War Leader*. London: The Hambledon Press, 1994.

Chandler, David. *The Campaigns of Napoleon*. New York: Macmillan, 1966.

Chickering, Roger. *Imperial Germany and a World Without War: The Peace Movement and German Society, 1892–1914*. Princeton: Princeton University Press, 1975.

Churchill, Winston S. *The Unknown War: The Eastern Front*. New York: Charles Scribner's Sons, 1932.

_____. *The World Crisis*. Vol. 1. New York: Charles Scribner's Sons, 1923.

von Clausewitz, Carl. *On War*, edited and translated by Michael Howard and Peter Paret. Princeton: Princeton University Press, 1976.

Craig, Gordon A. *The Battle of Königgratz*. Philadelphia: Lippincott, 1964.

_____. *The Politics of the Prussian Army, 1640–1945*. Oxford: Oxford University Press, 1955.

Crampton, R. J. *The Hollow Detente: Anglo-German Relations, 1911–1914*. London: George Prior, 1977.

Creveld, Martin van. *Supplying War: Logistics from Wallenstein to Patton*. Cambridge: Cambridge University Press, 1977.

Curtiss, Sheldon. *The Russian Army Under Nicholas I, 1825-1855*. Durham, N.Ca.: Duke University Press, 1965.

Dedijer, Vladimir. *The Road to Sarajevo*. New York: Simon and Schuster, 1966.

Deutschmann, Wilhelm. "Die militärischen Massnahmen in Österreich-Ungarn während der Balkankriege 1912–1913." Ph.D. diss., University of Vienna, 1966.

Earle, Edward Mead, editor. *Makers of Modern Strategy*. Princeton: Princeton University Press, 1971.

Ernharth, Ronald Louis. "The Tragic Alliance: Austro-German Military Cooperation, 1871–1918." Ph.D. diss., Columbia University, 1970.

Falls, Cyril. *The Great War*. New York: Capricorn Books, 1961.

Farrar, L. L. *The Short-War Illusion*. Oxford: Oxford University Press, 1973.

Fischer, Fritz. *Germany's Aims in the First World War*, translated by Marian Jackson. New York: W. W. Norton, 1967.

———. *War of Illusions: German Policies from 1911 to 1914*, translated by Marian Jackson. New York: W. W. Norton, 1975.

French, David. *British Economic and Strategic Planning, 1905-1915*. London: Allen and Unwin, 1982.

———. *British Strategy and War Aims, 1914–1916*. London: Allen and Unwin, 1986.

Fry, Michael G. *Lloyd George and Foreign Policy*. Vol 1, *The Education of a Statesman, 1890–1916*. Montreal: McGill-Queen's University Press, 1977.

Führ, Christoph. *Das K.u.K. Armeeoberkommando und die Innenpolitik in Oesterreich, 1914–1917*. Graz: Böhlau, 1968.

Fuller, Jr. William C. *Civil-Military Relations in Imperial Russia, 1881–1914*. Princeton: Princeton University Press, 1985.

———. *Strategy and Power in Russia, 1600–1914*. New York: Free Press, 1992.

von Glaise-Horstenau, Edmund. *Franz Josephs Weggefährte: Das Leben des Generalstabschefs Grafen Beck*. Vienna: Amalthea Verlag, 1930.

Glückmann, Karl. *Das Heerwesen der österreichisch-ungarischen Monarchie*. Vienna: Seidel und Sohn, 1911.

Gooch, G. P. *History of Modern Europe, 1878–1919*. New York: Henry Holt, 1923.

Gray, Colin S. *Strategic Studies: A Critical Assessment*. Westport, Conn.: Greenwood Press, 1982.

Grigg, John. *Lloyd George: From Peace to War, 1912–1916*. Berkeley: University of California Press, 1985.

Halpern, Paul G. *The Mediterranean Naval Situation, 1908–1914*. Cambridge: Harvard University Press, 1971.

Hantsch, Hugo. *Leopold Graf Berchtold: Grandseigneur und Staatsmann*. Graz: Verlag Styria, 1963.

Helmreich, Ernst Christian. *The Diplomacy of the Balkan Wars*. Cambridge: Cambridge University Press, 1938.

Horvath, F. *Captured*. New York: Dodd and Mead, 1930.

Howard, Michael. *The Franco-Prussian War*. London: Rupert Hart-Davies, 1961.

Jarausch, Konrad H. *The Enigmatic Chancellor: Bethmann Hollweg and the Hubris of Imperial Germany*. New Haven, Conn.: Yale University Press, 1973.

Jaszi, Oscar. *The Dissolution of the Habsburg Monarchy*. Chicago: University of Chicago Press, 1961.

Joll, James. *The Origins of the First World War*. London: Longman, 1984.

Käs, Ferdinand. "Versuch einer zusammengefassten Darstellung der Tätigkeit des österreichisch-ungarischen Generalstabes in der Zeit von 1906 bis 1914 unter besonderer Berücksichtung der Aufmarschplanungen und Mobilmachungen." Ph.D. diss., University of Vienna, 1962.

Keiger, John F. V. *France and the Origins of the First World War*. New York: St. Martin's Press, 1983.

Kennedy, Paul. *The Rise and Fall of the Great Powers: Economic Change and Military Conflict from 1500 to 2000*. New York: Random House, 1987.

————, editor. *The War Plans of the Great Powers, 1880–1914*. London: George Allen and Unwin, 1979.

Kessel, Eberhard. *Moltke*. Stuttgart: K. F. Koehler Verlag, 1957.

Kissinger, Henry. *Diplomacy*. New York: Simon and Schuster, 1994.

Kiszling, Rudolf. *Erzherzog Franz Ferdinand von Oesterreich Este*. Graz: Böhlau, 1952.

Krauss, Alfred. *Moltke, Benedek und Napoleon*. Vienna: L. W. Seidel und Sohn, 1901.

Kuhn, Thomas S. *The Structure of Scientific Revolutions*. Chicago: University of Chicago Press, 1970.

Lambi, Ivo Nikolai. *The Navy and German Power Politics, 1862–1914*. Boston: Allen and Unwin, 1984.

Langer, William L. *European Alliances and Alignments, 1871–1890*, 2d ed. New York: Alfred A. Knopf, 1966.

Lebow, Richard Ned. *Nuclear Crisis Management: A Dangerous Illusion*. Ithaca, N.Y.: Cornell University Press, 1987.

Liddell Hart, B. H. *The Real War*. Boston: Little, Brown, 1930.

Lieven, D.C.B. *Russia and the Origins of the First World War*. New York: St. Martin's Press, 1983.

Luvaas, Jay. *The Military Legacy of the Civil War*. Chicago: University of Chicago Press, 1959.

Macartney, C. A. *The Habsburg Empire, 1790–1918*. New York: Macmillan, 1969.

McDonald, David MacLaren. *United Government and Foreign Policy in Russia, 1900–1914*. Cambridge: Harvard University Press, 1992.

Markus, Georg. *Der Fall Redl*. Vienna: Amalthea Verlag, 1984.

März, Eduard. *Austrian Banking and Financial Policy: Creditanstalt at a Turning Point, 1913–1923*, translated by Charles Kessler. London: Weidenfeld and Nicolson, 1984.

May, Arthur. *The Hapsburg Monarchy, 1867–1914*. Cambridge: Harvard University Press, 1968.

May, Ernest R., editor. *Knowing One's Enemies: Intelligence Assessments Before the Two World Wars*. Princeton: Princeton University Press, 1984.

Meyer, Bradley J. "Operational Art and the German Command System in World War I." Ph.D. diss., Ohio State University, 1988.

Mueller, John. *Retreat From Doomsday: The Obsolescence of Major War*. New York: Basic Books, 1989.

Offer, Avner. *The First World War: An Agrarian Interpretation*. Oxford: Clarendon Press, 1991.

Pantenius, Hans Jürgen. *Der Angriffsgedanke gegen Italien bei Conrad von Hötzendorf*. Vienna: Böhlau, 1983.

Paret, Peter, editor. *Makers of Modern Strategy*. Princeton: Princeton University Press, 1986.

Petre, Francis Lorraine. *Napoleon and the Archduke Charles*. London: Boadley Head, 1909.

von Pitreich, Max Freiherr. *1914: Die militärischen Probleme unseres Kriegsbeginnes*. Vienna: Selbstverlag, 1934.

_____. *Lemberg 1914*. Vienna: Verlag von Adolf Holzhausens Nachfolger, 1929.

Porch, Douglas. *The March to the Marne: The French Army, 1871–1914*. Cambridge: Cambridge University Press, 1981.

Porter, Bruce D. *War and the Rise of the State: The Military Foundations of Modern Politics*. New York: The Free Press, 1994.

von Preradovich, N[icholas]. *Die Führungsschichten in Oesterrieich und Preussen*. Wiesbaden: Steiner, 1955.

Pribram, Alfred F. *Austrian Foreign Policy, 1908–1918*. London: George Allen and Unwin, 1923.

Regele, Oskar. *Feldmarschall Conrad: Auftrag und Erfüllung, 1906–1918*. Vienna: Herold Verlag, 1955.

Remak, Joachim. *The Origins of World War I, 1871–1914*. New York: Holt, Rinehart and Winston, 1967.

_____. *Sarajevo*. New York: Criterion Books, 1959.

Reynolds, David. *Britannia Overruled: British World Policy and World Power in the Twentieth Century*. London: Longman, 1991.

Ritter, Gerhard. *The Schlieffen Plan: Critique of a Myth*. New York: Praeger, 1958.

_____. *The Sword and the Scepter*. 4 Vols. Miami, Fla.: University of Miami Press, 1970.

Ropponen, Risto. *Die russische Gefahr: Das Verhalten der öffentlichen Meinung Deutschlands und Österreich-Ungarns gegenüber der Aussenpolitik Russlands in der Zeit zwischen dem Frieden von Portsmouth und dem Ausbruch des Erstens Weltkriegs*. Helsinki: Suomen Historiallinen Seura, 1976.

Rothenberg, Gunther E. *The Army of Francis Joseph*. West Lafayette, Ind.: Purdue University Press, 1976.

Schlichting, Friedrich. *Moltke und Benedek: Eine Studie über Truppenführung*. Berlin: E. S. Mittler und Sohn, 1900.

Schmitt, Bernadotte E. *The Annexation of Bosnia, 1908–1909*. Cambridge: Cambridge University Press, 1937.

Seton-Watson, R. W. *Sarajevo*. London: Hutchinson, 1925.

Setzen, Joel A. "The Doctrine of the Offensive in the French Army on the Eve of World War I." Ph.D. diss., University of Chicago, 1972.

Shanafelt, Gary W. *The Secret Enemy: Austria-Hungary and the German Alliance, 1914–1918*. New York: Columbia University Press, 1985.

Showalter, Dennis E. *Railroads and Rifles: Soldiers, Technology, and the Unification of Germany*. Hamden, Conn.: Archon Books, 1975.

_____. *Tannenberg: Clash of Empires*. Hamden, Conn.: Archon Books, 1991.

Snyder, Jack. *The Ideology of the Offensive: Military Decision Making and the Disasters of 1914*. Ithaca, N.Y.: Cornell University Press, 1984.

von Staabs, Hermann. *Aufmarsch nach zwei Fronten: Auf Grund der Operationspläne von 1871–1914*. Berlin: E. S. Mittler und Sohn, 1925.

Steiner, Zara S. *Britain and the Origins of the First World War*. New York: St. Martin's Press, 1977.

Stern, Fritz. "Bethmann Hollweg and the War: The Limits of Responsibility." In *The Responsibility of Power*, edited by Leonard Krieger and Fritz Stern. Garden City, N.Y.: Doubleday, 1967.

Stone, Norman. *The Eastern Front, 1914–1917*. New York: Charles Scribner's Sons, 1975.

_____ . *Europe Transformed, 1878–1919*. Cambridge: Harvard University Press, 1984.

Taylor, A.J.P. *The Struggle for Mastery in Europe, 1848–1918*. New York: Oxford University Press, 1971.

_____ . *War by Timetable: How the First World War Began*. London: Macdonald, 1969.

Tuchman, Barbara. *The Guns of August*. New York: Macmillan, 1962.

Tunstall, Graydon A. *Planning for War Against Russia and Serbia: Austro-Hungarian and German Military Strategies, 1871–1914*. Boulder, Colo.: Social Science Monographs, 1993.

Turner, L.C.F. *Origins of the First World War*. New York: Norton, 1970.

von Urbanski, August. *Conrad von Hötzendorf: Soldat und Mensch*. Vienna: Ulrich Moser, 1938.

Vermes, Gabor. *István Tisza: The Liberal Vision and Conservative Statecraft of a Magyar Nationalist*. New York: East Euopean Monographs, Columbia University Press, 1985.

Wallach, Jehuda L. *The Dogma of the Battle of Annihilation: The Theories of Clausewitz and Schlieffen and Their Impact on the German Conduct of Two World Wars*. Westport, Conn.: Greenwood Press, 1986.

Wank, Solomon. "Aehrenthal and the Policy of Action." Ph.D. diss., Columbia University, 1961.

Wedel, O. H. *Austro-German Diplomatic Relations, 1908–1914*. Stanford: Stanford University Press, 1932.

Williamson, Samuel R. *Austria-Hungary and the Origins of the First World War*. New York: St. Martin's Press, 1991.

_____ . *The Politics of Grand Strategy: Britain and France Prepare for War, 1904–1914*. Cambridge: Harvard University Press, 1969.

Wilson, Keith M. *The Policy of the Entente: Essays on the Determinants of British Foreign Policy, 1904–1914*. Cambridge: Cambridge University Press, 1985.

Zeman, Z.A.B. *The Break-Up of the Habsburg Monarchy, 1914–1918*. New York: Oxford University Press, 1961.

von Zwehl, H. *Erich von Falkenhayn*. Berlin: E. S. Mittler und Sohn, 1926.

Zweig, Stefan. *The World of Yesterday*. New York: Viking Press, 1943.

ARTICLES

Armour, Ian D. "Colonel Redl: Fact and Fantasy." *Intelligence and National Security*, 2, 1 (1987).

Auffenberg-Komarow, Moritz. "Conrad von Hötzendorf." In *Neue österreichische Biographie*. Vol. 3. Vienna: Amalthea Verlag, 1926.

Bairoch, P. "Europe's Gross National Product: 1800–1975." *Journal of European Economic History*, 5 (1976).

Balogh, Eva. "The Turning of the World: Hungarian Progressive Writers on the War." *The Habsburg Empire in World War I*. New York: Columbia University Press, 1977.

Bridge, F. R. "The British Declaration of War on Austria-Hungary in 1914." *The Slavonic Review*, 47 (1969).

Collins, D.N. "The Franco-Russian Alliance and Russian Railways, 1891–1914." *The Historical Journal*, 16 (1973).

Craig, Gordon. "Delbrück: The Military Historian." In *Makers of Modern Strategy*, edited by Edward Mead Earle. Princeton: Princeton University Press, 1971.

Dedijer, Vladimir. "Sarajevo Fifty Years After." *Foreign Affairs*, 42, 4 (1964).

Dockrill, M. L. "David Lloyd George and Foreign Policy Before 1914." In *Lloyd George: Twelve Essays*, edited by A.J.P. Taylor. New York: Atheneum, 1971.

Epstein, Klaus. "German War Aims in the First World War." *World Politics*, 15, 1 (1962).

van Evera, Stephen. "The Cult of the Offensive and the Origins of the First World War." *International Security*, 9, 1 (1984).

Fischer, Fritz. "The Miscalculation of English Neutrality: An Aspect of German Foreign Policy on the Eve of World War I." In *The Mirror of History: Essays in Honor of Fritz Fellner*, edited by Solomon Wank. Santa Barbara, Calif.: ABC-Clio, 1988.

Fuller, William C. "The Russian Empire." In *Knowing One's Enemies: Intelligence Assessment Before the Two World Wars*, edited by Ernest R. May. Princeton: Princeton University Press, 1984.

Gasser, Adolf. "Deutschlands Entschluss zum Präventivkrieg 1913–1914." In *Discordia Concors: Festschrift für Edgar Bonjour*, edited by Marc Sieber. Basel: Helbing and Lichtenhahn, 1968.

———. "Der deutsche Hegemonialkrieg von 1914." In *Deutschland in der Weltpolitik des 19. und 20. Jahrhunderts: Festschrift für Fritz Fischer*, edited by Imanuel Geiss and Bernd Jürgen Wendt. Düsseldorf: Bertelsmann Universitätsverlag, 1973.

Gilbert, Bentley B. "Pacifist to Interventionist: David Lloyd George in 1911 and 1914. Was Belgium the Issue?" *The Historical Journal*, 28, 4 (1985).

Golovin, N. "The Great Battle of Galicia (1914): A Study in Strategy." *The Slavonic Review*, 5 (1926/1927).

Herwig, Holger H. "Disjointed Allies: Coalition Warfare in Berlin and Vienna, 1914." *The Journal of Military History*, 54 (1990).

———. "From the Tirpitz Plan to Schlieffen Plan: Some Observations on German Military Planning." *The Journal of Strategic Studies*, 9, 1 (1986).

Höbelt, Lothar. "Schlieffen, Beck, Potiorek und das Ende der gemeinsamen deutsch-österreichisch-ungarischen Aufmarschpläne im Osten." *Militärgeschichtliche Mitteilungen*, 2 (1984).

Holborn, Hajo. "Moltke and Schlieffen: The Prussian-German School." In *Makers of Modern Strategy*, edited by Edward Mead Earle. Princeton: Princeton University Press, 1971.

Howard, Michael. "Men against Fire: The Doctrine of the Offensive in 1914." In *Makers of Modern Strategy*, edited by Peter Paret. Princeton: Princeton University Press, 1986.

Jarausch, Konrad. "The Illusion of Limited War: Chancellor Bethmann Hollweg's Calculated Risk, July 1914." *Central European History*, 2 (1969).

Kagan, Donald. "World War I, World War II, World War III." *Commentary*, 84, 3 (1987).

Kaiser, David E. "Germany and the Origins of the First World War." *Journal of Modern History*, 55, 3 (1983).

Kann, Robert A. "Emperor William II and Archduke Francis Ferdinand in Their Correspondence." *The American Historical Review*, 57, 2 (1952).

_____. "Trends in Austro-German Literature During World War I: War Hysteria and Patriotism." In *The Habsburg Empire in World War I*. New York: Columbia University Press, 1977.

Kaufman, Robert G. " 'To Balance or To Bandwagon?' Alignment Decisions in 1930s Europe." *Security Studies*, 1, 3 (1992).

Kennedy, Paul. "The First World War and the International Power System." *International Security*, 9, 1 (1984).

Lebow, Richard Ned. "Windows of Opportunity: Do States Jump Through Them?" *International Security*, 9, 1 (1984).

von Lengyel, General Bela. "Die oesterreichisch-ungarische Heeresleitung 1914." *Allgemeine Schweizerische Militärzeitschrift* (1964).

Levy, Jack S. "Preferences, Constraints, and Choices in July 1914." *International Security*, 15, 3 (1990/91).

Maier, Charles S. "Wargames: 1914–1919." *The Journal of Interdisciplinary History*, 18, 4 (1988).

May, Ernest R. "Cabinet, Tsar, Kaiser: Three Approaches to Assessment." In *Knowing One's Enemies: Intelligence Assessment Before the Two World Wars*. Princeton: Princeton University Press, 1984.

Palmer, R. R. "Frederick the Great, Guibert, Bülow: From Dynastic to National War." In *Makers of Modern Strategy*, edited by Edward Meade Earle. Princeton: Princeton University Press, 1943.

Palumbo, Michael. "German-Italian Military Relations on the Eve of World War I." *Central European History*, 12, 4 (1979).

Peball, Kurt. "Der Feldzug gegen Serbien und Montenegro in Jahre 1914." *Oesterreichische Militärische Zeitschrift*, special issue 1 (1965).

Remak, Joachim. "1914—The Third Balkan War: Origins Reconsidered." *Journal of Modern History*, 43 (1971).

Ritter, Gerhard. "Die Zusammenarbeit der Generalstäbe Deutschlands und Oesterreich-Ungarns vor dem ersten Weltkrieg." In *Zur Geschichte und Problematik der Demokratie: Festgabe für Hans Herzfeld*. Berlin: Duncker und Humblot, 1958.

Röhl, J.C.G. "Admiral von Müller and the Approach of War, 1911–1914." *Historical Journal*, 12, 4 (1969).

Rothenberg, Gunther E. "The Austro-Hungarian Campaign Against Serbia in 1914." *The Journal of Military History*, 53, 2 (1989).

_____. "Der Fall 'U': Die geplante Besetzung Ungarns durch die k.u.k. Armee im Herbst 1905." *Schriften des Heeresgeschichtlichen Museums in Wien*, 4 (1969).

_____. "Moltke, Schlieffen, and the Doctrine of Strategic Envelopment." In *Makers of Modern Strategy*, edited by Peter Paret. Princeton: Princeton University Press, 1986.

————. "Toward a National Hungarian Army: The Military Compromise of 1868 and Its Consequences." *Slavic Review*, 31 (1972).

Rudel, Colonel Rudolf. *Streffleurs Militärische Zeitschrift*, 1 (1912).

Sagan, Scott D. "1914 Revisited: Allies, Offense, and Instability." *International Security*, 11, 1 (1986).

Schorske, Carl. "Politics and the Psyche in *fin de siècle* Vienna: Schnitzler and Hofmannsthal." *American Historical Review*, 66, 2 (1961).

Schroeder, Paul. "World War I as Galloping Gertie: A Reply to Joachim Remak." *The Journal of Modern History*, 44 (1972).

Schweller, Randall L. "Bandwagoning for Profit: Bringing the Revisionist State Back In." *International Security*, 19, 1 (1994).

Showalter, Dennis E. "The Eastern Front and German Military Planning, 1871–1914: Some Observations." *East European Quarterly*, 15, 2 (1981).

————. "German Grand Strategy: A Contradiction in Terms?" Militärgeschicht-liche Mitteilungen (1990).

Sked, Alan. "A Patriot for Whom?" *History Today*, 36 (1986).

Snyder, Jack. "Civil-Military Relations and the Cult of the Offensive, 1914 and 1984." *International Security*, 9, 1 (1984).

Stern, Fritz. *Gold and Iron: Bismarck, Bleichröder, and the Building of the German Empire*. New York: Knopf, 1977.

Stöckelle, Gustav. "Der Feldzug von Limanova-Lapanow 1-20. Dezember 1914." *Österreichische Militärische Zeitschrift*, 1 (1965).

Stone, Norman. "Army and Society in the Habsburg Monarchy, 1900–1914." *Past and Present*, 33 (1966).

————. "Austria-Hungary." In *Knowing One's Enemies: Intelligence Assessment Before the Two World Wars*, edited by Ernest R. May. Princeton: Princeton University Press, 1984.

————. "Conrad von Hötzendorf." *History Today*, 13 (1963).

————. "Hungary and the Crisis of July 1914." *Journal of Contemporary History*, 1, 3 (1966).

————. "Die Mobilmachung der österreichisch-ungarischen Armee 1914." *Militär-geschichtliche Mitteilungen*, 2 (1974).

————. "Moltke-Conrad: Relations Between the Austro-Hungarian and German General Staffs, 1909–1914." *The Historical Journal*, 9, 2 (1966).

Trumpener, Ulrich. "War Premeditated? German Intelligence Operations in July 1914." *Central European History*, 9 (1976).

Vann, James Allen. "Hapsburg Policy and the Austrian War of 1809." *Central European History*, 7 (1974).

Wank, Solomon. "Some Reflections on Conrad von Hötzendorf and His Memoirs based on Old and New Sources." *Austrian History Yearbook*, 1 (1965).

Williamson, Samuel R. "Influence, Power, and the Policy Process: The Case of Franz Ferdinand, 1906–1914." *The Historical Journal*, 17 (1974).

————. "The Origins of World War I." *Journal of Interdisciplinary History*, 18, 4 (1988).

————. "Theories of Organizational Process and Foreign Policy Outcomes." In *Diplomacy: New Approaches in History, Theory, and Policy*, edited by Paul Gordon Lauren. New York: The Free Press, 1979.

Wilson, K. M., "Understanding the 'Misunderstanding' of 1 August 1914." *The Historical Journal*, 37, 4 (1994).

Young, Harry F. "The Misunderstanding of August 1, 1914." *Journal of Modern History*, 48, 4 (1976).

Index

About the Author

JOHN H. MAURER is Associate Professor in the Strategy Department of the U.S. Naval War College where he lectures on naval history and strategy, international history, and strategic studies. He is also the assistant editor of the journal *Diplomacy and Statecraft*.

ISBN 0-275-94998-2

9 0 0 0 0>

EAN

9 780275 949983

HARDCOVER BAR CODE